# Diplomacy and Deterrence

Zia Ul Haque Shamsi

# Diplomacy and Deterrence

## Blending D2 to Achieve Peace, Stability, and Security

New York · Berlin · Bruxelles · Chennai · Lausanne · Oxford

Library of Congress Cataloging-in-Publication Data

Names: Shamsi, Zia Ul Haque, author.
Title: Diplomacy and deterrence : blending D2 to achieve peace, stability, and security / Zia Ul Haque Shamsi.
Description: New York : Peter Lang Publishing, Inc., 2024. | Includes bibliographical references.
Identifiers: LCCN 2024039972 (print) | LCCN 2024039973 (ebook) | ISBN 9781636679204 (paperback) | ISBN 9781636679181 (ebook) | ISBN 9781636679198 (epub)
Subjects: LCSH: Conflict management. | Security, International. | War—Prevention. | Diplomacy. | Deterrence (Strategy)—Political aspects. | World politics—21st century.
Classification: LCC JZ5595 .S53 2024  (print) | LCC JZ5595  (ebook) | DDC 327.2—dc23/eng/20241024
LC record available at https://lccn.loc.gov/2024039972
LC ebook record available at https://lccn.loc.gov/2024039973
DOI 10.3726/ b22396

Bibliographic information published by the Deutsche Nationalbibliothek.
The German National Library lists this publication in the German
National Bibliography; detailed bibliographic data is available
on the Internet at http://dnb.d-nb.de.

Cover design by Peter Lang Group AG

ISBN 9781636679204 (paperback)
ISBN 9781636679181 (ebook)
ISBN 9781636679198 (epub)
DOI 10.3726/b22396

© 2024 Peter Lang Group AG, Lausanne
Published by Peter Lang Publishing Inc., New York, USA
info@peterlang.com - www.peterlang.com

All rights reserved.
All parts of this publication are protected by copyright.
Any utilization outside the strict limits of the copyright law, without the permission of the publisher, is forbidden and liable to prosecution.
This applies in particular to reproductions, translations, microfilming, and storage and processing in electronic retrieval systems.

This publication has been peer reviewed.

Dedicated to the people around the world who make sincere efforts for global peace, stability, and security

*Ten years of Talk is better than One Day of War*

Andrei Gromyko

*War causes Deaths, Destruction, Devastation, Division, and Displacement (D5)*
*Peace ensures the Likelihood of Life, Liberty, Love, Living, and Longevity (L5)*
***Therefore,***
*Do anything but avert the Next War*

Zia Ul Haque Shamsi

# CONTENTS

|  |  |  |
|---|---|---|
|  | Acknowledgments | xi |
|  | List of Abbreviations | xiii |
| Introduction |  | 1 |
|  | Central Argument | 5 |
|  | Significance of the Subject | 5 |
|  | Plan of the Book | 5 |
|  | Conclusion | 9 |
| Chapter 1 | Theoretical Precepts | 11 |
|  | Introduction | 11 |
|  | Realism: Power and Security | 12 |
|  | Peace: The Ultimate Objective of Diplomacy? | 14 |
|  | Stability: A Precursor for Progress and Development | 16 |
|  | Security: One Word, Many Shades | 18 |
|  | Deterrence: Understanding and Execution | 20 |
|  | Strategic Culture: Understanding in Its Essence | 22 |
|  | Conclusion | 23 |

| | | |
|---|---|---|
| Chapter 2 | Analytical Tools and Models | 29 |
| | Introduction | 29 |
| | Possibility-Probability (P2) Model | 29 |
| | Diplomacy and Deterrence (D2) Model | 31 |
| | C7 Model | 33 |
| | Conclusion | 36 |
| Chapter 3 | Avenues of Diplomacy | 39 |
| | Introduction | 39 |
| | Geo-diplomacy | 40 |
| | External Relations (Primary and Foremost) | 41 |
| | Economic Diplomacy | 42 |
| | (Defense) Military Diplomacy | 43 |
| | Religious/Ideological Diplomacy | 46 |
| | Public Diplomacy | 48 |
| | Cultural Diplomacy | 50 |
| | Sports Diplomacy | 52 |
| | Regional Diplomacy | 53 |
| | International Diplomacy | 55 |
| | Conclusion | 55 |
| Chapter 4 | Significance of Diplomacy as a Tool for Peace, Stability, and Security | 59 |
| | Introduction | 59 |
| | Diplomacy and its Nuances | 61 |
| | Positive Diplomacy | 62 |
| | Negative Diplomacy | 64 |
| | Hybrid Mannerism of Diplomacy | 66 |
| | International Forums for Common Good | 67 |
| | Conclusion | 71 |
| Chapter 5 | Avenues of Deterrence | 75 |
| | Introduction | 75 |
| | Conventional Deterrence | 76 |
| | Nuclear Deterrence | 77 |
| | Extended Deterrence | 79 |
| | Ideological Deterrence | 80 |
| | Economic Deterrence | 82 |

|  |  |  |
|---|---|---|
|  | Colonial Deterrence | 83 |
|  | Cultural Deterrence | 84 |
|  | Regional Deterrence | 86 |
|  | International Deterrence | 87 |
|  | Geopolitical Deterrence | 87 |
|  | Conclusion | 88 |
| Chapter 6 | Efficacy of Deterrent Capability as a Guarantor of Peace, Stability, and Security | 91 |
|  | Introduction | 91 |
|  | Deterrence: What Is It? | 92 |
|  | Nuclear Deterrence: Averting Wars to Dare Not | 95 |
|  | Nuclear Deterrent Capability: A Guarantor of National Security? | 97 |
|  | Capability | 98 |
|  | Capacity | 98 |
|  | Credibility | 99 |
|  | Communicability | 100 |
|  | Command | 100 |
|  | Control | 100 |
|  | Conduct | 100 |
|  | Capability | 101 |
|  | Capacity | 102 |
|  | Credibility | 103 |
|  | Communicability | 103 |
|  | Command | 104 |
|  | Control | 104 |
|  | Conduct | 104 |
|  | Conclusion | 104 |
| Chapter 7 | Inseparable Linkage between Diplomacy and Deterrence | 107 |
|  | Application of the P2 Model (Initiators/Attackers) | 109 |
|  | Interdependence of Diplomacy and Deterrence | 120 |
|  | Conclusion | 121 |
|  | Conclusion | 123 |
|  | Bibliography | 129 |

# ACKNOWLEDGMENTS

By the Grace of Allah, my fourth international book, on an extremely important subject is before you. I bow my head Before Allah Almighty for His Countless Blessings upon me during the entire period of this research. The purpose of writing on the subject is to reemphasize the need to avoid wars and conflicts, particularly between the Unequal Military Powers (UMPs) where the stronger states cause deaths and destruction in the relatively weaker states.

I am indebted to all academics, and practitioners from military, diplomatic, and civilian bureaucracy, whose talks, lectures, and writings have benefitted me immensely in shaping my research on this most compelling subject. An effort has been made to acknowledge and refer to their work appropriately; however, if any idea or work is not referred to properly, I would seek guidance to make suitable corrections. Some of the ideas presented in this book may have been published in my weekly columns in *Daily Times, Pakistan*, and/or in my earlier publications while this book was under review, however, the same has been referred, to wherever needed.

I am also grateful to *Peter Lang* for their continued support in the completion of this important project. The idea is to generate discussions, deliberations, and awareness, and contribute to averting the next war, particularly against the relatively smaller and weaker states.

Once again, many thanks to all my family members for supporting me in my academic endeavors.

# LIST OF ABBREVIATIONS

| | |
|---|---|
| **ABM** | Anti-Ballistic Missile |
| **ACDA** | Arms Control and Disarmament Affairs (Pakistan) |
| **APT** | Advanced Persistent Threats |
| **AEC** | Atomic Energy Commission |
| **AER** | Atomic Energy Research |
| **AG** | Australia Group |
| **AGPL** | Actual Ground Position Line |
| **AJK** | Azad Jammu & Kashmir |
| **AP** | Additional Protocol |
| **ATGM** | Anti-tank Guided Missile |
| **BECA** | Basic Exchange and Cooperation Agreement (India-US) |
| **BJP** | Bhartiya Janta Party |
| **BMD** | Ballistic Missile Defense |
| **BoP** | Balance of Power |
| **BOT** | Build-Operate-Transfer |
| **C&C** | Command and Control |
| **CANDU** | Canada Deuterium Uranium |
| **CBM** | Confidence-Building Measure |
| **CD** | Conference on Disarmament |

| | |
|---|---|
| CENTO | Central Treaty Organization |
| CFL | Cease-Fire Line |
| CGS | Chief of General Staff |
| CIA | Central Intelligence Agency |
| CIR | Canada-India Reactor |
| CI | Critical Infrastructure |
| CIP | Critical Infrastructure Protection |
| CMC | Cuban Missile Crisis |
| CNS | Centre for Non-proliferation Studies |
| COAS | Chief of Army Staff |
| COMCASA | Communications, Compatibility and Security Agreement (India-US) |
| CPEC | China-Pakistan Economic Corridor |
| CSI | Container Security Initiative |
| CTBT | Comprehensive Test Ban Treaty |
| CTR | Cooperative Threat Reduction |
| CWC | Chemical Weapons Convention |
| CNI | Clean Network Initiative |
| CS | Cybersecurity |
| CSBM | Confidence and Security-Building Measures |
| CSCO | Cyber Security Coordination Office |
| DCC | Defense Committee of Cabinet |
| DG | Director General |
| DGMO | Director General Military Operations |
| DOD | Department of Defense (US) |
| DPRK | Democratic People's Republic of Korea |
| DTD | Director of Technical Development |
| DU | Dual Use |
| EURATOM | European Atomic Energy Community |
| ECHR | European Court of Human Rights |
| EC | European Community |
| EXBS | Export Control and Related Border Security Assistance |
| ED | Existential Deterrence |
| EEZ | Exclusive Economic Zone |
| ENDC | Eighteen Nations Disarmament Committee |
| ERL | Engineering Research Laboratories |
| EU | European Union |
| EXCOMM | Executive Committee of the National Security Council |

| | |
|---|---|
| FBI | Federal Bureau of Investigation |
| FCNA | Force Command Northern Areas |
| FDO | Flexible Deterrent Options |
| FFAO | Future Framework Alliance Operation |
| FGA | Fighter Ground Attack |
| FIFA | Federation Internationale de Football Association |
| FMCT | Fissile Material Cut-off Treaty |
| FSS | Full-Scope Safeguards |
| FOBs | Forward Operating Bases |
| G7 | Group of Seven |
| GCC | Gulf Cooperation Council |
| GDP | Gross Domestic Product |
| GHQ | General Headquarters |
| GOC | General Officer Commanding |
| GP | Global Partnership |
| GPM | Governmental Policy Model |
| HEU | Highly Enriched Uranium |
| HT | Hybrid Threats |
| HW | Hybrid Warfare |
| IBM | International Business Machines Corporation |
| ICC | International Criminal Court |
| ICJ | International Court of Justice |
| ICRC | International Committee of the Red Cross |
| ICS | Industrial Control Systems |
| ICT | Information and communication technology |
| IDF | Israel Defence Forces |
| IHL | International Humanitarian Law |
| ILC | International Law Commission |
| IS | Islamic State |
| ISIL | Islamic State of Iraq and the Levant |
| ISIS | Islamic State of Iraq and Syria |
| IT | Information Technology |
| IAEA | International Atomic Energy Agency |
| ISA | Industrial Security Agreement (India-US) |
| IAEC | Indian Atomic Energy Commission |
| IAF | Indian Air Force |
| ICBM | Inter-continental Ballistic Missile |
| ICTP | International Center for Theoretical Physics |

| | |
|---|---|
| IGMDP | Integrated Missile Development Program |
| IHK | Indian Held Kashmir |
| INF | Intermediate-Range Nuclear Forces Treaty |
| INMM | Institute of Nuclear Materials Management |
| IR | International Relations |
| IRBM | Intermediate-Range Ballistic Missile |
| IISS | International Institute for Strategic Studies, London |
| ISI | Inter-Service Intelligence |
| IWT | Indus Water Treaty |
| J & K | Jammu and Kashmir |
| JeM | Jaish-e-Mohammad |
| JuD | Jamaat-ud-Dawa |
| KANUPP | Karachi Nuclear Power Plant |
| KRL | Khan Research Laboratory |
| KT | Kiloton |
| LeT | Lashkar-e-Toiba |
| LOAC | Law of Armed Conflict |
| LEMOA | Logistics Exchange Memorandum of Agreement (India-US) |
| LoC | Line of Control |
| LTBT | Limited Test Ban Treaty |
| MNC | Multinational Company |
| MoD | Ministry of Defense |
| MoU | Memorandum of Understanding |
| MRBM | Medium-Range Ballistic Missile |
| MTCR | Missile Technology Control Regime |
| MENA | Middle East and North Africa |
| MPECI | Military, Political, Economic, Civil, and Intelligence |
| MS | Member States |
| NAM | Non-aligned Movement |
| NATO | North Atlantic Treaty Organization |
| NCA | National Command Authority |
| NCSS | National Cyber Security Strategy |
| NDU | National Defense University |
| NMD | National Missile Defense |
| NNSA | National Nuclear Security Administration (US) |
| NNWS | Non-nuclear Weapons State(s) |
| NLI | Northern Light Infantry |
| NSA | Non-State Actors |

| | |
|---|---|
| NPCIL | Nuclear Power Corporation of India Ltd. |
| NPR | Nuclear Posture Review |
| NPT | Nuclear Non-proliferation Treaty |
| NPTRC | Non-proliferation Treaty Review Conference |
| NSAP | National Security Action Plan |
| NSG | Nuclear Suppliers Group |
| NTI | Nuclear Threat Initiative |
| NWD | Non-weaponized Deterrence |
| NWFZ | Nuclear Weapons Free Zone |
| NWFZSA | Nuclear Weapons Free Zone in South Asia |
| NWS | Nuclear Weapons State(s) |
| NGO | Non-governmental Organization |
| NIAP | National Information Assurance Policy |
| NIC | National Intelligence Council |
| NICE | National Institute for Health and Care Excellence |
| OAS | Organization of American States |
| OCHA | UN Office for the Coordination of Humanitarian Affairs |
| OBM | Organizational Behavior Model |
| OSCE | Organization for Security and Cooperation in Europe |
| PAEC | Pakistan Atomic Energy Commission |
| PAL | Permissive Action Link (Security device for nuclear weapons) |
| PAF | Pakistan Air Force |
| PAROS | Prevention of an Arms Race in Outer Space |
| PARR | Pakistan Research Reactor |
| PECI | Political, Economic, Civil, and International |
| PIDC | Pakistan Industrial and Technical Centre |
| PMSEII | Political, Military, Social, Economic, Information, and Infrastructure |
| PPC | Permanent Population Committee |
| PPP | Public-Private Partnership |
| PNE | Peaceful Nuclear Explosion |
| PNRA | Pakistan Nuclear Regulatory Authority |
| PNSRP | Pakistan Nuclear Safety and Radiation Protection (Ordinance 1984 and Regulation 1990) |
| P2 | Possibility-Probability |
| PSI | Proliferation Security Initiative |
| PTBT | Partial Test Ban Treaty |
| QCB | Qatar Central Bank |

| | |
|---|---|
| Q-CERT | Qatar Computer Emergency Response Team |
| QNA | Qatar News Agency |
| RAP | Readiness Action Plan |
| SA | State Actors |
| SCADA | Supervisory Control and Data Acquisition |
| SEA | Syrian Electronic Army |
| SOP | Strategic Operating Plans |
| SPSS | Statistical Package for the Social Sciences |
| TEU | Treaty on European Union |
| UAE | United Arab Emirates |
| UK | United Kingdom |
| UN | United Nations |
| UNCLOS | United Nations Convention on the Law of the Sea |
| UNDP | UN Office for the Coordination of Humanitarian Affairs |
| UNSC | United Nations Security Council |
| US | United States |
| USSR | Union of Soviet Socialist Republics |
| VJTF | Very High Readiness Joint Task Force |
| WTO | World Trade Organization |
| RAM | Rational Actor Model |
| R&D | Research and Development |
| RoK | Rann of Kutch |
| SAARC | South Asian Association for Regional Cooperation |
| SALT | Strategic Arms Limitation Talks |
| SAM | Surface-to-Air Missile |
| SCI | Security Container Initiative |
| SEATO | Southeast Asia Treaty Organization |
| SECDIV | Strategic Export Control Divisions |
| SFCD | Strategic Force Communication Planning |
| SRBMs | Short-Range Ballistic Missiles |
| SLBM | Submarine-Launched Ballistic Missile |
| SPD | Strategic Plans Division (Pakistan) |
| SOPs | Standard Operating Procedures |
| SRAM | Short-Range Attack Missile |
| SRO | Statutory Regulatory Orders |
| SSG | Special Services Group |
| SSOD | Special Session on Disarmament |
| START | Strategic Arms Reduction Talks |

| | |
|---|---|
| **TIFR** | Tata Institute of Fundamental Research |
| **TMD** | Theater Missile Defense |
| **UAV** | Unmanned Aerial Vehicle |
| **UE** | Uranium Enrichment |
| **UF6** | Uranium Hexafluoride |
| **UKAEA** | United Kingdom Atomic Energy Agency |
| **UN** | United Nations |
| **UNCLOS** | United Nations Convention on Law of the Sea |
| **UNSC** | United Nations Security Council |
| **UNSCR** | United Nations Security Council Resolution |
| **WA** | Wassenaar Arrangement |
| **WD** | Weaponized Deterrence |
| **WMD** | Weapons(s) of Mass Destruction |
| **ZC** | Zangger Committee |

# INTRODUCTION

The title of the book is indicative of the significance of the two terms or tools the states have, diplomacy and deterrence, to protect and promote their interests and ensure their territorial integrity and sovereignty. If diplomacy uses the soft power of the state to prevail over an opponent, it needs the strong backing of the hard power to ensure that the adversary is convinced about the effectiveness of the deterrent value the state has. Likewise, the deterrent value of the state must be complemented by the skillful deployment of diplomacy so that wars and conflicts are averted. However, the efficacy of the two, diplomacy and deterrence, in attaining, maintaining, and sustaining peace, stability, and security is highly dependent on the skillful employment of diplomacy and the effective deployment of the deterrent value each state may have depending on its capacity to project its power. Since the two tools, diplomacy and deterrence, have nearly similar objectives; attaining, maintaining, and sustaining peace, stability, and security, therefore, they must be employed in a hybrid manner either concurrently or sequentially to achieve the desired objectives seamlessly and efficiently.

There is little doubt that given the objectives in the respective domains, diplomacy and deterrence, will have to complement each other to ensure that the other one delivers. For instance, an imminent war can be averted through proactive and intense diplomacy even if the deterrence has failed, however, the probability of a military engagement will increase manifolds if both diplomacy and deterrence fail to deliver. Therefore, it is necessary that at least one must deliver to avoid wars and conflicts, however, to attain, maintain, and sustain peace, stability, and security, both diplomacy and deterrence will have to deliver. This author opines that the hybrid employment of diplomacy and deterrence may be the most suitable manner to achieve the desired results.

Perhaps the most prudent quote to avoid war and attain, maintain, and sustain peace, stability, and security comes from the erstwhile Soviet leader Andre Gromyko "Ten years of negotiations are better than one day of war."[1] Gromyko was a long-term (1957–1985) Soviet foreign minister and the architect of the Communist regime's Cold War policy, and this line from him calls for a thorough analysis of the Soviet Union's Cold War policies even after the passage of over seven decades. Russian diplomats still believe in Gromyko's philosophy regarding diplomacy and still quote him. "For 25 years, the Minister for Foreign Affairs in the Soviet Union was Andrei Gromyko, and he used to say about the Iraq-Iran war—it is better to have ten years of negotiations than one day of war. He was and is still right—it is essential to understand that hostilities and war cannot solve anything. All the wars end with peace, so we should start with peace."[2]

Inspired by Gromyko's dicta, this author opines that since war causes deaths, destruction, devastation, division, and displacement (5-Ds and all of these have negative connotations), whereas peace ensures the likelihood of a better life, liberty, love, living, and longevity (5-Ls and all of these have positive connotations), therefore, global stakeholders must try to anything but avert the next war.

Briefly, diplomacy forms the essential element of human relationships: personal, groups, communities, or the states. According to Britannica, diplomacy is "the established method of influencing the decisions and behavior of foreign governments and peoples through dialogue, negotiation, and other measures short of war or violence."[3] Whereas, National Geography defines diplomacy as "the art and science of maintaining peaceful relationships between nations, groups, or individuals. Often, diplomacy refers to representatives of different groups discussing such issues as conflict, trade, the environment, technology, or security."[4] Another definition suggests that "Diplomacy is the art, the science, and how nations, groups, or individuals conduct their affairs, in ways to safeguard their interests and promote their political, economic, cultural or scientific relations, while maintaining peaceful relationships."[5] Another definition reads, "diplomacy can be defined as a process between actors (diplomats, usually representing a state) who exist within a system (international relations) and engage in private and public dialogue (diplomacy) to pursue their objectives peacefully."[6]

The concept of deterrence dates to the creation of mankind because it aims to quell greed, and access by one person, group, or state against all of the others. However, the strategy for its execution has evolved and is reflective of politico-military, and socio-cultural methodologies of dealing with wars and conflicts.

Lawrence Freedman writes, "The first words used, spoken by God to man, contain a deterrent threat."[7] Likewise, Muslim's Holy Book Al-Quran also laid great emphasis on the utmost preparation to respond to the infidels. "*And prepare against them what force you can and horses tied at the frontier, to frighten/ deter thereby the enemies of Allah and your enemies and others besides them, whom you do not know (but) Allah does know . . .*"[8] This implies that "Operational Preparedness" by a state under threat must be to its fullest capacity, and its only purpose should be to deny the enemy its mischievous and unjust objectives.

The Chinese sage Sun Tzu's insistence on utmost preparations for war also leads to a similar concept. Sun Tzu, some 2,500 years ago cautioned that one must not spend energies to think whether his enemy would attack him or not, but rather invest your efforts in the preparation of such defensive mechanisms that the enemy does not even contemplate an offensive action for the fear of unfavorable consequences.[9] However, the age-old concept became a central piece to academic writings and military preparedness with the introduction of nuclear weapons as an instrument of threat to deny the enemy the use of military power in the nuclearized environment.[10] Therefore, the race to acquire nuclear weapons capability began when the world saw its immense destructive power over the Japanese cities of Hiroshima and Nagasaki on the fateful days of August 6 and 9, 1945.

Interestingly, Britannica's definition closely aligns with an established understanding of deterrence that warrants a favorable response by the opponent. This is perhaps one reason that two concepts or processes, diplomacy and deterrence, have inseparable linkages, and if anyone is deficient in a state's security architecture, wars, and conflicts become more imminent. However, it is necessary to mention that deterrence is not only deployed in wars and conflicts but in all such situations where a favorable response is desired from a non-compliant state. This may be in the domain of human rights, women empowerment, child labor, female education, information freedom, the right to vote, democratic processes, and even restrictions in the release of financial support for the violations of international laws, norms, and good practices.

The international system is anarchic according to the realist paradigm. The states are not equal in geographical size, population strength, natural resources, economic prowess, technological progress, and military strength. Therefore, wars and conflicts are inevitable because states are selfish and greedy, and want more power for prestige, and security.

This author opines that the states have at least two major tools at their disposal to make their place among the comity of nations: diplomacy and deterrence. While diplomacy aims to protect and promote a country's national interests, deterrence serves as an armed guard to ensure the territorial integrity and sovereignty of the state by deterring the opponents of dire consequences in case of any misadventures. In that context, states must strive to expand their power base on each front: diplomacy and deterrence.

States do enhance their stature by adopting diplomatic approaches through investments in education, health, environment, culture, sports, tourism, and contributions to peace, stability, and security. Several states around the world may not have strong deterrents through their military strengths but have very persuasive diplomatic approaches. Switzerland, New Zealand, Qatar, and many other states that are much smaller in size and military strengths carry a lot of weight in international affairs due to their conduct through diplomacy.

On the other hand, some states strive to enhance their deterrent value by showing force with their military strengths. States can enhance their deterrent value which can be calculated based on C7 (Capability, Capacity, Credibility, Communicability, Command, Control, and Conduct) and the political will. However, the states that rely only on the physical and material strengths of their military alone may not have political or economic clout that may earn them respect among the comity of nations. The Soviet Union lost its political identity while it had one of the strongest militaries of the time. Iraq was reduced to its size when it had the largest military in the region. Pakistan is a nuclear-armed state and contributes a maximum number of men to UN Peacekeeping forces, but its economy is dependent on support from international institutions.

Since the nature and character of wars and conflicts have evolved over the decades due to technological progress and cyber and space are the likely battlefields in the decades to come, therefore, states must strive to expand their diplomatic approaches and concurrently enhance their deterrent value to attain, maintain, and sustain peace, stability, and security in the region and beyond.

## Central Argument

Under the realist paradigm, wars and conflicts between states with protracted conflicts and active disputes are possible with a higher degree of probability. However, this becomes inevitable if the essential tools of diplomacy and deterrence, which every state has, to further its interests and guard its frontiers, fail to achieve their objectives. If at least one of these tools: diplomacy and deterrence can deliver, there is a relatively medium probability of averting a war, because a state's deterrent value is enhanced by C7 plus the political will, and its international stature is regarded due to its diplomatic advances. However, if both are working, there is an even higher probability of attaining, maintaining, and sustaining peace, stability, and security in the region and beyond.

## Significance of the Subject

The 21st-century wars have destroyed smaller countries due to wars between UMPs. This is happening primarily because the smaller states do not carry a deterrent value, and do not have a worthwhile diplomatic approach. It is argued in this book that wars can be averted if any of the two: diplomacy and deterrence are working between the stakeholders. Therefore, it is extremely important to contextualize the significance and essentiality of deploying diplomacy and deterrence in sync to avert wars and conflicts, particularly between UMPs.

## Plan of the Book

The book deals with all aspects related to diplomacy and deterrence as essential tools to attain, maintain, and sustain efforts for peace, stability, and security. For this purpose, this author sets the scene against the backdrop of Chinese sage Sun Tzu's precepts that refer to deterrence by utmost preparation to meet an eventuality.

The Introduction highlights the significance of the employment of diplomacy and deterrence in a hybrid manner either concurrently or sequentially to achieve the desired objectives of attaining, maintaining, and sustaining peace, stability, and security in the region and beyond. It will also focus on the basic definitions of the main components: diplomacy and deterrence, however, the specific and focused details on diplomacy and deterrence will be discussed in the following chapters.

Chapter 1, *Theoretical Precepts* is aimed at developing the understanding and awareness about the interdependence and inseparability of diplomacy and deterrence for attaining, maintaining, and sustaining peace, stability, and security, first at the regional, and then expanding it to the global level. *Theoretical Precepts* will contextualize the important strategic terminologies to the subject of debate: realism, peace, stability, security, deterrence, and strategic culture. The present international system is deeply indebted to the age-old theoretical precepts the academics and the practitioners are jealously guarding, particularly the shades of classical realism. This author also shows his disappointment with the increasing number of wars and conflicts between the UMPs primarily under the realm of national interests which is the cornerstone of realism.

Chapter 2, *Analytical Tools and Models*, defines and explains the several academic tools and models developed by this author for different studies. However, few of these models are being deployed in this research to validate the argument that if diplomacy and deterrence are deployed in a hybrid manner, they can be more effective in attaining, maintaining, and sustaining peace, stability, and security in the region and beyond.

First, the *C7 Model* (Capability, Capacity, Credibility, Communicability, Command, Control, and Conduct). This model or the appraisal tool will help in determining the strengths and weaknesses of any state from the perspective of being an attacker or a defender. The C7 evaluation is supported by a strong political will which helps in deciding about the military operations by the practitioners. Second, the possibility-probability (P2) Model, can be used for scenario building and decision-making based on the evaluation of states' capabilities, both military and non-military, done in the C7 Model. Finally, the Diplomacy-Deterrence (D2) Model will help in determining the effectiveness of the response of the defender. Remember, the primary objective must remain the avoidance of war, particularly between the UMPs.

Therefore, this chapter aims to explain the various analytical tools and academic models to review some of the contemporary wars and conflicts of the 21$^{st}$ century to determine the efficacy of diplomacy and deterrence in attaining, maintaining, and sustaining peace, stability, and security at all levels.

Chapter 3, *Avenues of Diplomacy*, deals with the range of diplomatic options from economic to military, and socio-cultural to ideological diplomacy, as tools to further the state's national interests and prevail upon its opponents using diplomatic overtures. Diplomacy, as a tool to further the state's interests, has endless possibilities. It has a role to play in every domain of the state: external relations, governance, commerce and trade, economy and development, lawfare, and even sports. Therefore, this chapter is aimed at venturing into the avenues of diplomacy to determine its significance and efficacies in attaining, maintaining, and sustaining peace, stability, and security at the regional level and expanding it further at the global level.

Chapter 4, the significance of diplomacy as an essential tool to strive for peace, stability, and security, across regions and the globe cannot be overemphasized. Therefore, the chapter *Significance of Diplomacy as a Tool for Peace, Stability, and Security* debates the two shades of diplomacy: positive and negative, with certain examples. For instance, the positive role of the US in South Asia but the negative in the Middle East. On several occasions, the US was instrumental in averting a near-war situation between the two nuclear neighbors: India and Pakistan. But the US continues to Veto UNSC Resolutions for a ceasefire in Gaza where Israel is committing genocide of the Palestinian people. Considering positive and negative diplomacy by certain states at different times, perhaps in line with their self-interests, the chapter will conclude the debate on the essentiality of diplomacy to attain, maintain, and sustain global peace, stability, and security.

Chapter 5, *Avenues of Deterrence*, deals with the range of avenues in which the concept of deterrence in theories, from classical deterrence to ready deterrence, and from rational deterrence to all-spectrum deterrence, and in practice, to find the best option for attaining, maintaining, and sustaining global peace, stability, and security. Neither the concept nor its application is new in the international system which is based on an anarchic system deeply rooted in a realist's paradigm of power and security. Still, the concept remains at the center of academic debates and draws a wide-ranging interest among researchers. Therefore, this chapter aims to highlight all the avenues of deterrence: conventional, nuclear, ideological or religious, economic, colonial, and cultural, as has been practiced historically by states, either singly or in combination, to achieve their stated objectives.

Chapter 6, *Efficacy of Deterrent Capability as a Guarantor of Peace, Stability, and Security* will review the different capabilities of the stakeholders to determine its efficacy in delivering peace, stability, and security at the regional as well as the global level. Because deterrence remains one of the most practiced military strategies in all its avenues, and therefore, this author is not deploying nuclear deterrence alone in the discussion. While Non-Kinetic Warfare (NKW) has gained more popularity in military strategy in the changed paradigm, economic deterrence through engagement and sanctions has assumed a leading role in punishing the target state. For this purpose, the author lays great emphasis on evaluating a state's deterrent value to determine whether, in times of crisis, it will be of some help or not.

Chapter 7, *The Inseparable Linkage between Diplomacy and Deterrence*, will deliberate on the significance and essentiality of both these tools in attaining, maintaining, and sustaining global peace, stability, and security. Also, several wars and conflicts of the 21$^{st}$ century will be tested on Possibility-Probability (P2) and Diplomacy and Democracy (D2) Models to prove the central argument. This author opines that diplomacy, and deterrence can deliver the stated objectives of attaining, maintaining, and sustaining peace, stability, and security at the regional and global levels when deployed in synergy and relentlessly. Both these tools are not a given and therefore have to be always pursued skillfully to get the desired results. If deterrence is not permanent and needs to be updated and upgraded, diplomacy also needs to explore more and more avenues and options to bargain one's position with the opponents because each state is working to further its national interests and therefore it would be naive to expect the other extending concessions without any worthwhile gains.

The *conclusion* will sum up the book and present its findings on whether the hybrid employment of diplomacy and deterrence can attain, maintain, and sustain peace, stability, and security at the regional and global level. This author is of the view that deterrence alone cannot guarantee peace, stability, and security. Therefore, it is reemphasized that a strong diplomatic effort, well supported by a host of elements of soft power will be needed to attain, maintain, and sustain peace, stability, and security. The same had been missing in several countries in the conflict-ridden regions: South Asia, the Middle East, Europe, and now Africa, which is on the verge of a full-fledged war over Niger, at the time of this submission.

## Conclusion

During the research, an effort was made to study the wars and conflicts of the 21$^{st}$ century. To maintain originality and objectivity, the wars and conflicts from different regions and differing characters were deployed on a variety of research models/tools to examine the motives of the aggressors and the response of the defenders. The potential results or the outcomes of the research and observations have been presented in different tables to make the readers quickly grasp the outcome.

This author opines that diplomacy, and deterrence can work at their best when deployed in a hybrid manner: all avenues at all times and both bilaterally as well as multilaterally. While diplomacy and deterrence are working in the Korean Peninsula to avert military engagements between the aggressor North Korea and the responder South Korea, it did not work in Europe. Ukraine was unable to stop the Russian invasion even with the full support of NATO.

On the other hand, Qatar was able to avert a near-war by a much stronger KSA-led quartet that imposed an unjust blockade against a relatively much smaller brotherly neighbor in the Gulf. In Qatar's case, diplomacy took the lead role followed closely by its enhanced deterrent value due to its alliances with Turkey and the US. Therefore, it is incumbent upon relatively smaller states to deploy diplomacy and deterrence in a hybrid manner to draw maximum benefits to protect and promote their national interests and the primary objective must remain an avoidance of war that too against UMPs.

The hybrid employment of diplomacy and deterrence is not only needed to avert wars and conflicts but also to achieve multiple objectives in different domains. For instance, states may use the capability to coerce another state to submit to its demands to vote for it at regional and international forums. The same can be done to achieve a favorable outcome in bilateral agreements to draw maximum benefits out of the relatively weaker opponent. The greedy states following the precepts of realism can make use of their capability to even higher gains by compelling the other states to submit to their will.

This author opines that power is only an enabler, projected to ensure security, but its aim remains the fulfillment of national interests to achieve the national objectives in multiple domains which includes influencing the behavior of the other states. This is how realists justify their relevance in the international system, and that is why the relatively smaller states remain at the mercy of global leaders, and Institutions.

## Notes

1. Andre Gromyko is quoted by this author from multiple sources.
2. Ambassador Popov at the 4th International Media Forum of Journalists from Muslim Countries for Partnership of Civilizations, May 6, 2018, https://www.dhakatribune.com/world/145028/%E2%80%98it-is-better-to-have-ten-years-of-negotiations (accessed February 27, 2024).
3. https://www.britannica.com/topic/diplomacy (accessed July 9, 2023).
4. https://education.nationalgeographic.org/resource/diplomacy/ (accessed July 9, 2023).
5. https://www.cyber-diplomacy-toolbox.com/Diplomacy.html (accessed July 9, 2023).
6. Stephen McGlinchey, Diplomacy, January 8, 2017, E-International Relations, https://www.e-ir.info/2017/01/08/diplomacy/ (accessed July 9, 2023).
7. Lawrence Freedman, *Deterrence* (Cambridge: Polity Press, 2004), 7.
8. Al-Quran Ul Kareem, Surah Anfal (8), Verse 60 (Madinah Munawwarah: Shah Fahad Quran Sharif Printing Complex, 1993), 244.
9. Sun Tzu, *The Art of War*, ed. James Clavell (Lahore: Combine Printers, 1983), 83.
10. Bernard Brodie, ed., *The Absolute Weapon* (New York: Harcourt, Brace & Company, 1946), 69.

# · 1 ·
# THEORETICAL PRECEPTS

## Introduction

The two subjects, diplomacy and deterrence, have been at the center of debate for a long time, as precursors to peace, stability, and security at all levels: national, regional, and global. However, despite a clear understanding of these concepts, there has been no respite from wars and conflicts in any region of the world. The uncertainty, instability, and complexity in the management and resolution of wars and conflicts have deepened, and therefore the frequency of physical violence, particularly between the UMPs, has increased manifold. The situation is compounded by the introduction of disruptive technologies and the formation of newer blocs which is reverting the existing international system from unipolarity to multipolarity.

This book is aimed at developing an understanding and awareness of the essentiality of blending diplomacy and deterrence to attain, maintain, and sustain peace, stability, and security, first at the regional level, and then expanding to the global level. Therefore, this chapter will review and dwell on the theoretical aspects deployed in the following chapters.

## Realism: Power and Security

Realism proffers that the international system is anarchic, consisting of independent political entities referred to as states,[1] which remain the central element. Therefore, for its survival among the comity of nations, each state organizes a diplomatic effort in different states and international organizations to further their interests, and the primary purpose remains the accomplishment of peace. Likewise, each state ensures a minimum level of deterrent value so that it can thwart any potential threat,[2] meaning the purpose is to deter the opponent from any undesired actions.

Realism does not stop here, because states are pursuing the precepts related to power and security. Under the same premise, it is assumed that states adopt a rational approach to sustain themselves as a sovereign unit in the prevalent environment.[3] Realism remains one of the most practiced international relations theories because its precepts have survived over centuries.[4] Realism has been relentlessly examined by renowned academics like Kenneth Waltz's defensive realism and Mearsheimer's offensive realism, which have been instrumental in understanding the complexities of achieving global peace and hence motivated this author to introduce the terminology of nonviolent peace. Realism's focus on conflicts and state power aligns it with military strategic issues more than anything else,[5] in which deterrence must play an important role.

The golden precepts of realism date back to the era of Thucydides[6] and Chanakya Kautilya,[7] progressing through the Middle Ages by Machiavelli.[8] However, Thomas Hobbes[9] in the 17th century, and Hans Morgenthau[10] in the previous century have been influential in shaping the policies of Western democracies.

Thucydides, who studied the Peloponnesian Wars (431–404 BC), viewed bilateral relations between states as competitive because of the natural differences between states' interests. He is rightly recognized as the founder of classical realist theory, which dilates upon the "security and survival are the primary values and war is the final arbiter."[11] Whereas the Chinese sage, Sun Tzu had some different ideas about wars and conflicts. He prophesied that wars must be won without fighting, and if wars become imminent, efforts must be made to achieve a quick victory and avoid protracted military engagements.

Contrarily, Machiavelli emphasized enhancing the power of the prince so that he can serve his people with immunity. He thought that the prince must exploit all resources available to him to acquire power. He cautioned the prince about the threats and the opportunities available to him and advised him to take initiative for the purpose and be prepared for any eventualities in the process.[12] However, Hobbes opined that the "International state of nature is a condition of actual or potential war; there can be no permanent or guaranteed peace between sovereign states. War is necessary, as a last resort, for resolving disputes between states that cannot agree and will not acquiesce."[13]

The previous century saw Hans Morgenthau insisting on the innate desire of humans to dictate their terms on the potential opponents which naturally led to disagreements, and conflicts often leading to wars.[14] On the other hand, Kenneth Waltz opined that states strive to remain viable while remaining in the existing system.[15] That may be achieved through the balance of power or by joining a powerful bloc in the evolving world order. However, the fundamental argument of Waltz remains on a formal structure of any international system and not based on human nature alone, primarily because the states do not conduct their operations in isolation. In Waltz's view, the international system during the Cold War era was more stable due to bipolarity. Therefore, he opined that defensive realism argues for the state's desire to survive, for which it acquires power either on its own or by aligning itself with any other powerful bloc.[16]

The precepts related to *Balance of Power* (BoP) rest on maintaining equilibrium in the existing international system. However, the premise for the effectiveness of BoP rests on the efficiency and flexibility of the alliances in shaping the environment best suited to its collective interests. In this process, even a single state can play the all-important role of a balancer, though it remains immeasurable.[17]

On the other hand, defensive realists think that a disorder creates a negative perception of the preparatory actions of another state thus creating a potential threat. This situation is referred to as a security dilemma because the relatively smaller states are not certain about the intention of the other state. For this purpose, states at times do adopt and execute actions that may be referred to as expansionist or revisionist primarily to enhance their security. Examples of defensive realism include the offense-defence theory by Robert Jervis,[18] and Stephen Van Evera,[19] the balance-of-power theory by Barry Posen,[20] and the balance-of-threat theory by Stephen Walt,[21] alongside the security dilemma theory.[22] This particular situation calls for enhancing the state's deterrent capability to ensure that the adversary is kept away from any misadventure, and a non-violent peace is maintained, at least.

On the other hand, the offensive realists give diagnostic prevalence to the aggressive and ruthless international system as the primary reason for the multiple conflicts between the two states or the group of states. The proponents of offensive realism believe that anarchy allows the revisionist state to expand its area of influence. To increase the area of influence both in the political and military domain, states strive to increase their relative power to ensure their survival and influence in the region and beyond. However, states do evaluate the costs and benefits of such an expansionism before they execute their plans.[23] However, offensive realists, do not subscribe to the idea of the historic dominance of hegemons in a regional security complex and the potential reactions of the relatively smaller states to a potential regional hegemon-like bandwagoning.[24] John Mearsheimer opines that "[t]he international system competes until the great powers achieve the status of a regional hegemon the best state for any great power. This is done through aggressive behavior."[25]

Realists profess that the status quo can be sustained if the *BoP* is instituted for which an offense-defense balance must be ensured. However, this author agrees with Stephen that dominance in the domain of offensive actions would reflect that subjugation is not difficult for the attackers, whereas a solid defense would make the attacker's actions far more challenging.[26] This means that the warring states must be aware of each other's evolving capabilities by evaluating the deterrent value so that the policy formulation and the response strategy adequately cater to potential and perceived threats.

The realist's thoughts helped determine the conduct of the bigger states because they took advantage of their strength to make smaller states comply with their dictates. This situation makes the environment tenser, and the non-violent peace may turn into a violent battleground.

## Peace: The Ultimate Objective of Diplomacy?

There is little doubt that the easiest way to resolve the dispute is to silence the opponent, especially if it is weaker physically, and win the argument. However, this strategy of silencing the adversary through brute force is now met with greater resistance even from UMPs. This does not mean that relatively stronger nations are willing to largely change their strategy, but certainly, adopt a range of non-kinetic options before putting the boots on the ground.

Global affairs continue to be governed under the cloud of realism, which calls for power and security, even at the cost of slicing the resources of the neighboring states. The colonial era is replete with examples of territorial capture of the natural resources by the relatively stronger nations.

The beauty of social sciences lies in its disagreements and divergent views. Be it the theorists, academics, or practitioners, there is little probability that each of these communities will come on the same page without conflictual ideas. There are no universal definitions of strategic terminologies of common use: peace, conflict, extremism, terrorism, deterrence, security, etc. Because the understanding of the context in which these terminologies are referred is largely influenced by the socio-cultural environment, politico-economic settings, and the geostrategic calculus. Consequently, it is understandable that there are disagreements, not only on the definitions and understandings but also on the responses by the stakeholders. Therefore, it is necessary to first look at the linguistic definitions given in credible dictionaries, and then turn toward the academic explanations. According to Cambridge, peace is "freedom from war and violence, especially when people live and work together happily without disagreements . . ."[27] Whereas, as per Britannica, peace is "a state in which there is no war or fighting."[28]

Looking at these dictionary meanings, defining peace appears a relatively simple affair, but this author would not subscribe to the mere absence of war as peace, because peace has a multitude of dimensions, and therefore must not be looked at through the lens of wars and conflicts alone.

In an era where non-kinetic applications are becoming much easier and cost-effective tools, the absence of war would not mean peace. Pakistan suffered under the cloud of hybrid warfare from India for over two decades now and a period of no war is usually referred to as no peace as well.

Peace as an issue of personal rights must be extended to the communities, states, regions, and ultimately at the global level. Because it is not only the organized violence that disrupts the peace but also the evolving issues such as pandemics, global warming due to climatological changes, non-proliferation of lethal weapons, militarization of space, recurrent refugee crises, unresolved disputes between the states that may stress on the peace efforts of global institutions.

Peace is perhaps the most desired entity for an individual, group, state, region, and universal. However, its price has escalated over time. The Military Industrial Complex (MICs) of the developed West does not allow a prolonged period of peace in conflict zones: Middle East, South Asia, and now in Europe as well. The true meaning of peace for the Iraqis, Libyans, Syrians, Yemenis, Afghans, and now Ukrainians, is meaningless.

The concepts of social and societal peace remain in academic writings only, especially for the developing nations, many of them are faced with wars and conflicts with UMPs. Every state makes a National Security Policy (NSP), some announce it and some keep it confidential, for unknown reasons. However, we do not see a declaratory National Peace Policy by any state, either in the developed world or among the developing nations.

This author opines that total peace in its true sense may not be attained, maintained, and sustained if the states are under the cloud of realism because peace is not a given thing, it needs a deliberate policy, strategy, and effort. However, with the successful exploitation of acquired or available tools like diplomacy and deterrence, wars can be averted, and non-violent peace can be achieved.

## Stability: A Precursor for Progress and Development

Defining stability is even more complex because it calls for an international system based on stable structures. Stability at the national, regional, and global levels cannot be achieved under the clouds of realism, primarily because realism is based on power and security. Hence, the relationship between states cannot be stable in the presence of a fear of violence by the relatively bigger power, even if the probability is low.

Since states are not equal in size, population, natural resources, economic strengths, and military capability, therefore, an effective international system must provide some sanctity to the sovereign rights of each state, regardless of the abovementioned attributes.

For this purpose, an attempt was made soon after World War I (WW I). The League of Nations was established on January 10, 1920, to promote international cooperation leading to peace and stability.[29] Its headquarters was based in Geneva, and its core concepts were based on liberal philosophy including arms control, ensuring security and stability across all regions, letting diplomacy through negotiations to improve an overall security environment. However, it was bound to underperform in the realist paradigm, and it happened that way in the coming decades, as it failed to avert World War II (WW II).

Likewise, the United Nations (UN) was formally established on October 24, 1945, in the aftermath of WW II. It was hoped that the mistakes of the past would not be repeated and other wars of that dimension and destruction would be avoided. After 75 years of its formation, the UN successfully performs humanitarian assistance and other crises, however, it fails in averting wars between UMPs. Moreover, it continues to remain under the cloud of the developed West that was instrumental in its establishment.

Stability at any level; global or regional, cannot be attained, maintained, and sustained, unless the stakeholders have a reasonable understanding of each other's national interest, and a common framework of progress and development because states are not inherently equal. This author opines that Qatar's blockade by its much bigger and militarily stronger neighbors could be a good example of this argument. The Gulf Cooperation Council (GCC) as a sub-region of the Middle East is relatively affluent, and member states have common socio-cultural values. Yet, the blockade was executed for over three years to compel Qatar to comply with the demands of the relatively bigger neighbors, due to a lack of stability in regional structures.

The fundamentals of stable international systems may include a sense of equals, and mutual respect for common national interest, however, the same might not be possible under the realist paradigm, and therefore, stability in its true spirit may never see the light of the day. But that would not mean the end of efforts on the part of diplomacy as a tool to attain, maintain, and sustain stability at all levels.

At the regional and sub-regional level, states do have relevant organizations formed for the same purpose, but the furtherance of one's interest as proffered by the realist paradigm becomes the major impediment. However, if states can reach a common understanding that peoples' well-being remains the most important national interest and the same will be respected for other states in the region, regardless of the size and resources, there will be a relatively higher probability of achieving regional stability. Subsequently, the same model can be applied to expand the area of relative stability.

Moreover, stability has multiple avenues to deal with. Beginning with political stability to socio-cultural stability, and economic stability to security stability, each of these elements is extremely important for overall regional stability. The Association of Southeast Asian Nations (ASEAN) is a good example of a regional organization that is living up to its expectations and objectives. ASEAN members include Brunei Darussalam, Cambodia, Indonesia, Lao PDR, Malaysia, Myanmar, Philippines, Singapore, Thailand, and Vietnam. Though established on August 8, 1967, its Charter was officially enacted on December 15, 2008, with its Secretariat in Jakarta, Indonesia. It calls for mutual respect, non-interference, and commitment to the non-use of force to resolve any disputes among the member states.[30] The population of the entire region is religiously, ethnically, and culturally diverse, with nearly no signs of discontent. ASEAN is the best example of hybrid peace and productive engagement within and without.[31] Moreover, the ASEAN does not have a regional hegemon, though Indonesia is the most populace state and the largest Muslim country in the world. Brunei Darussalam is the smallest state and the richest, but none of the big player eyes on its wealth, as has been seen in other regions. Iraq's invasion of Kuwait may be referred to as a case in point. ASEAN's most significant achievement is "Asian economic integration, among Asia-Pacific nations to form one of the world's largest free trade blocs and signing six free trade agreements with other regional economies."[32]

On the other hand, The South Asian Association for Regional Cooperation (SAARC) was established on December 8, 1985, with its Secretariat in Kathmandu, Nepal. The member countries included: Bangladesh, Bhutan, India, the Maldives, Nepal, Pakistan, and Sri Lanka, as its founding members, however, Afghanistan joined the group in April 2007.[33] The purpose of SAARC had numerous noble objectives: "to promote economic growth, social progress and cultural development within the South Asia region."[34] Contrarily, it remains the most inefficient body due to the enduring rivalry between the two largest member states: India and Pakistan, and hence the South Asian sub-region remains the most unstable area due to the presence of protracted conflicts and unresolved active disputes: Jammu and Kashmir (J&K).

While stability in all its dimensions is extremely important, political and security stability carries the burden of ensuring regional stability to avert wars and conflicts and achieve non-violent peace, at least.

## Security: One Word, Many Shades

Security, like many other strategic terminologies, does not have an agreed definition, neither by academics nor by practitioners. However, one thing is relatively clearer in the changed paradigm that it does not necessarily mean physical security by the military force alone.

This author defines security using the Australian phrase "No Worries." The most demanding domains that have been added to the security list fall under the broad heading of human security, which has at least seven compelling elements: personal, community, political, economic, food, health, and environment.[35] The other important elements of security include military, space, and cyber. These elements of security are the primary responsibility of each sovereign state toward its citizens and residents.

The term "security" appears in almost every discussion that takes place in domestic politics, international forums, academic discourse, and bilateral relations. However, the concept remains in search of its true meaning primarily because its various definitions are ambiguous and mostly out of context.[36] According to Morgenthau, there are numerous dimensions of this term and the first and foremost of these is power,[37] which is vital for the survival of the state[38] as a sovereign country. Other related dimensions include war avoidance[39] and the least concerns about potential threats.[40] However, the threat perception largely depends on the evaluation of the deterrent value of the adversary by the people at the helm of affairs who keenly read the historical past as well as the behavior of the adversarial state.[41] Perhaps, the ongoing war between Russia and Ukraine is due to the same perception the Russian leadership had for NATO's ambitious expansion toward the east.

Therefore, the threats to the security of any state can only be rightly evaluated with the correct assessment of the deterrent value each state has. In the changed paradigm, security is more related to an individual because he or she is more than willing to sacrifice everything for it. Hence the concept of human security gained primacy over the state's security. When it comes to human security, it includes almost everything that may cause concerns for an individual's basic needs like health, education, economic needs, and even environmental protection.[42] However, security in all these domains cannot be achieved by individuals and therefore makes it essential that a collective effort is made to ensure societal security leading to traditional security for the state as well[43] because it cannot rendered irrelevant even if the paradigm has shifted more toward human security.[44]

Economic security affects individuals more than any other form and remains central to the state's preparation for any potential threats from relatively powerful adversaries. Hence the state's economy and its military security are inseparable. However, the states may face a security dilemma due to differing threat perceptions and war preparedness,[45] even if they do not intend to go into a conflict or physical violence, but minor incidents may result in an uncontrolled escalation due to misinterpretation of the perceived threats.[46]

In the same context, it is essentially required to define the conflict because it is an outcome of disagreement between two or more individuals, groups, or states, and remains so since time immemorial. Like security, conflict has also been defined differently by various authors including that "a conflict is the result of opposing interests involving scarce resources, goal divergence, and frustration."[47] This definition reflects what realists have professed on the primacy of states that whenever states have differing interests, a conflict may emerge and if not resolved at an early stage may grow to become a cause of a violent conflict. The situation may lead to a security dilemma and an unintended arms race will further compound the situation.[48]

The disagreements leading to conflict is possible at each level: individual, group, society, and the state. At each of these levels, the primary cause remains the control and expansion of available means to maximize power so that others can be influenced easily. However, "social conflict is the opposition between individuals and groups based on competing interests, different identities, and or differing attitudes."[49] The conflict between states has a much wider canvas and affects all residents of the state alike, and therefore needs to be managed effectively even if cannot resolved in an early timeframe. The differing nature of conflicts makes it possible to manage them through diplomacy and deterrence to reduce the probability of escalating to violence.

However. once the states fail to manage or resolve their conflicts, war may become imminent, and "wars involve the taking of territory, the eviction of inhabitants, the death of soldiers and civilians, the destruction of property, ... War is among the most destructive phenomena that one human group can inflict on another."[50] This author subscribes to this definition.

## Deterrence: Understanding and Execution

Deterrence remains an age-old strategy in warfare. Deterrence continues to be a strategy that has stood the test of time. However, in contemporary times, the strategy is often traced back to the development of nuclear weapons in 1945. Bernard Brodie asserted that "if aggressor feared retaliation in kind, he would not attack."[51] He also opined that "thus far the chief purpose of our military establishment has been to win wars. From now on its chief purpose must be to avert them."[52]

In the early stages of the nuclear age, deterrence was defined as discouraging someone from acting by instilling fear of the consequences of that action ... Deterrence is contingent upon both capabilities and the intentions of doing the needful.[53] However, deterrence is not automatic; it must be obtained and achieved through specific measures and actions. Furthermore, its effectiveness varies and is not universally applicable.

According to Henry Kissinger,

> Deterrence is the attempt to keep an opponent from adopting a certain course of action by posing risks which will seem to him out of proportion to any gains to be achieved.... The higher the stakes, the more absolute must be the threat of destruction which faces him... But, the reverse is also true; the smaller the objective, the less should be the sanction.[54]

However, as far as its effectiveness is concerned, it is assumed that it remains the safest strategy even if the inventory of nuclear weapons is not too large.[55] To ensure its efficacy as a strategy, deterrence can be employed for war avoidance as well as influencing the opponent. Nuclear weapons on the inventory of any state give a lot more confidence to the leadership to set the parameters of the rules of engagement of its own.[56] Because deterrence is more effective if one can penetrate the decision-making processes of the enemy.[57]

Classical or rational deterrence theory is based on the principles of strategic parity and stability. It originates from power politics or political realism, which emphasizes the importance of maintaining a balance of power in the anarchic international system. According to the theory of balance of power, when the distribution of power among major nations is roughly equal, it promotes peace.[58]

Conversely, when significant asymmetries appear in the distribution of power resources, the likelihood of war significantly rises. Therefore, a nation whose power is growing will exploit its superior strength to potentially attack its now weaker adversaries.[59] Understandably, *Classical Deterrence Theory* theorizes increased chances of a violent conflict as and when the asymmetry reaches at alarming levels.[60] However, *Structural Deterrence Theory* accounts for a cost-benefit analysis and suggests the chances of violence increasing during asymmetry reduce when the cost of war increases beyond the capacity of the initiator.[61]

However, deterrence remains a function of convincing the enemies that your acts could be costlier than your gains. Yet some of the leading academics viewed that the proliferation of nuclear weapons would help states deter their potential enemies from waging wars against rivals.[62] This view supported relatively weaker and smaller states to acquire nuclear weapons to deter relatively bigger enemies.[63] However, this argument is based on the belief that the respective states will adopt a rational approach and a nuclear war will remain a far cry.[64]

However, deterrence has a very wide canvas, and its application is not restricted to the domain of wars and conflicts, even if it is employed to avoid wars in contemporary times. International organizations employ the concept against states that are non-compliant with the norms and practices desired by the system. For instance, the states that do not comply with human rights conventions are heavily sanctioned and may accept the terms and conditions to avert the sanctions. Likewise, financial institutions do have the leverage to impose penalties or discontinue support of states that employ child labor or do not follow the good practices of labor laws. Female education and women empowerment is also one area that draws the attention of international organizations and serves as a deterrent against non-compliant states. How effective these deterring measures are depends on the geopolitical considerations and socio-cultural aspects of the faltering states. For instance, the Taliban government in Afghanistan does not feel deterred when international institutions impose sanctions on the country for its denial of female education rights, unfortunately. Likewise, Pakistan was placed on the watch list by the Financial Action Task Force (FATF) for the lack of relevant laws to curb the money laundering that was allegedly used for terror financing. The requirement served as a deterrent and the country had to legislate the desired laws, rules, and regulations to recover out of the watch list.

Therefore, this author opines that even though the concept of deterrence is usually deployed to avert wars and conflicts, it can be effectively employed in all domains where the state is seen faltering on the international rules, regulations, norms, and good practices. To get the desired results if the concept of deterrence is deployed in a hybrid manner alongside proactive diplomacy with incentives and implications, there is a higher probability of attaining and maintaining the stated objectives.

## Strategic Culture: Understanding in Its Essence

The strategic culture of any society determines the modus operandi of its deterrent value. Strategic culture is shaped over decades or even over centuries by norms, practices, experiences, and expertise of the strategic community of society and serves as a beacon of credence for future generations. It determines how a particular state perceives security, and how it is going to respond to the impending threat. How the state prepares itself to meet evolving security challenges. Ken Booth also defined the strategic culture as "a nation's traditions, values, attitudes, patterns of behavior, habits, symbols, achievements and particular ways of adapting to the environment and solving problems concerning the threat and use of force."[65]

Therefore, the strategic culture of a particular state will determine how the state will deploy diplomacy and deterrence to attain, maintain, and sustain peace, stability, and security with its neighbors, either with disputes or conflicting interests. This is one reason why academia stresses understanding the strategic culture of a particular society and forewarns the practitioners before they choose war as a policy option. For instance, the successive US Administrations failed to understand the strategic culture of Afghanistan that it does not subscribe to foreign occupation and remained in the country for two decades before they were forced to leave. The same had happened to the erstwhile Soviet Union only over a decade ago, but both the superpowers of the time failed to understand the phenomenon of the strategic culture of Afghan society.

## Conclusion

The present international system is deeply indebted to the theoretical precepts mentioned in the above paragraphs and the academics and the practitioners are jealously guarding them, particularly the shades of classical realism. This author argues that the practice of age-old concepts has not helped in conflict management and resolution, and the wars and conflicts have increased both horizontally as well as vertically. There is no respite for mankind from the deaths and destruction in the 21$^{st}$ century as well, like before whereas the global issues that need to be addressed as a priority for the peoples' well-being have increased manifold. For instance, climate change, pandemics, rising inflation, diminishing energy resources, introduction of cyber warfare, etc. Therefore, it is incumbent upon global leaders and institutions to work relentlessly to attain, maintain, and sustain peace, stability, and security, at all levels. However, this author feels that it may not be possible until efforts are made to ensure that future wars and conflicts between the UMPs are averted using all available avenues of deterrence and diplomacy.

This chapter aimed to review the theoretical precepts related to the major subjects that are being debated in this book: peace, stability, security, diplomacy, and deterrence. The purpose was to maintain objectivity in developing the argument so that the efficacy of diplomacy and deterrence in attaining, maintaining, and sustaining peace, stability, and security can be ascertained at the regional level and beyond. Remember the ultimate objectives of these two elements of state, diplomacy, and deterrence remain to further the state's interests through the avoidance of wars and conflicts particularly between the UMPs.

However, it is necessary to mention that the end objective of international organizations and global stakeholders remains a peaceful, stable, and secure world where mankind can survive without the fears of being annihilated as has been the case in many ancient civilizations. This may sound too idealistic, but it is certainly doable through the employment of deterrence against the non-compliant states and proactive diplomacy to convince these states of unbearable consequences for the people and the state.

This author opines that power is only an enabler, projected to ensure security, but its aim remains the fulfillment of national interests to achieve the national objectives in multiple domains. This is how realists justify their relevance in the international system, and that is why the relatively smaller states remain at the mercy of global leaders, and Institutions. However, the desired objectives of peace, stability, and security can still be attained, maintained, and sustained in the region and beyond through the hybrid employment of diplomacy and deterrence. For instance, the Taliban government of Afghanistan is now not recognized by any other state except China, primarily due to its discriminatory policies toward female education and lack of women's rights to employment and expression. Yet, Afghanistan remains an important country because peace, stability, and security in the country are vitally important for the region and beyond.

## Notes

1 Robert Jackson and Georg Sorensen, *Introduction to International Relations: Theories and approaches*, 3rd ed. (Oxford: Oxford University Press, 2007), 60.
2 Hans Morgenthau, *Politics among Nations* (New York: Knopf, 1948), Chapters 1 and 2.
3 Ibid.
4 Charles W. Kegley Jr. and Eugene R. Wittkopf, *World Politics: Trends & Transformations*, 9th ed. (Belmont, CA: Thomson-Wadsworth, 2004), 31.
5 Robert Jervis, "Realism, Neoliberalism and Cooperation; Understanding the Debate," *International Security* 31, no. 4 (Summer 1999): 42–63.
6 Thucydides, an ancient Greek historian famous for his account of the Peloponnesian Wars between Athens and Sparta (431–404 BC).
7 Kautilya, a minister of the Maurya emperor of India, authored the seminal "Artha Shastra" which serves as the beacon of India's external policy over many centuries.
8 Niccolo Machiavelli, in "The Prince" (1532) laid great emphasis on the manifestation of power, and interests in managing the affairs of the state.

9 Thomas Hobbes, an English political philosopher whose famous book *Leviathan* established social contract theory in 1651.
10 Hanss Joachim Morgenthau, a leading scholar of international politics, developed the theory of political realism. His landmark work *Politics Among Nations*, was first published in 1948.
11 Robert Jackson and Georg Sorensen, *Introduction to International Relations: Theories and Approaches*, 3rd ed. (Oxford: Oxford University Press, 2007), 63.
12 Ibid., 64.
13 Ibid., 66.
14 Hanss J. Morgenthau, *Politics among Nations: The Struggle for Power and Peace*, 5th rev. ed. (New York: Alfred A. Knopf, 1978), 4–15.
15 See W. Julian Korab-Karpowicz, "Political Realism in International Relations," in *The Stanford Encyclopedia of Philosophy*, Summer 2013 ed., ed. Edward N. Zalta, http://plato.stanford.edu/archives/sum2013/entries/realism-intl-relations/ (accessed October 23, 2014).
16 Kenneth Waltz, *Theory of International Politics* (New York: McGraw Hill, 1979), 121.
17 See T.V. Paul, James J. Wirtz, and Michel Fortmann, ed., *Balance of Power: Theory and Practice in the 21$^{st}$ Century* (Stanford, CA: Stanford University Press, 2004).
18 Robert Jervis is one of the principal representatives of the Neorealist current within IR Theory.
19 Stephen Van Evera, "Offense, Defense, and the Causes of War," *International Security* 22, no. 4 (Spring 1998): 5–43.
20 Barry Posen, "The Security Dilemma and Ethnic Conflict," *Survival* 35, no. 1 (Spring 1993): 27–47.
21 Stephen M. Walt proposed "The balance of threat (BoT)" theory in an article titled "Alliance Formation and the Balance of World Power" in 1985. The balance-of-threat theory modified the popular balance-of-power theory in the neorealist school of international relations.
22 Jeffrey W. Taliaferro, "Security-Seeking Under Anarchy: Defensive Realism Reconsidered," *International Security* 25, no. 3 (Winter 2000/2001): 152–186.
23 John Mearsheimer, *The Tragedy of Great Power Politics* (New York: Norton, 2001), 139–161.
24 Jeffrey W. Taliaferro, "Security-Seeking Under Anarchy: Defensive Realism Reconsidered," *International Security* 25, no. 3 (Winter 2000/2001): 152–186.
25 John J. Mearsheimer, *The Tragedy of Great Power Politics* (New York: W.W. Norton, 2001), 21.
26 Stephen Van Evera, *Causes of War: Power and the Roots of Conflict* (Cornell: Cornell University Press, 1999), 117–192.
27 https://dictionary.cambridge.org/dictionary/english/peace (accessed July 12, 2023).
28 https://www.britannica.com/dictionary/peace (accessed July 12, 2023).
29 https://www.britannica.com/topic/League-of-Nations (accessed June 30, 2023).
30 https://asean.org/asean/about-asean/overview/ (accessed July 13, 2023).
31 The ASEAN has a few Buddhist nations, Muslim nations, and large Chinese and Hindu communities, but they live peacefully and participate in each other's socio-cultural functions enthusiastically.
32 Lindsay Maizland and Eleanor Albert, "What Is ASEAN," Council on Foreign Relations, https://www.cfr.org/backgrounder/what-asean (accessed April 12, 2021).

33 https://www.saarc-sec.org/ (accessed July 13, 2023).
34 South Asian Association for Regional Cooperation (SAARC), https://aric.adb.org/initiative/south-asian-association-for-regional-cooperation (accessed July 13, 2023).
35 UNDP Report, 1994.
36 Barry Buzan, *People, States, and Fear: The National Security Problems in International Relations* (Essck: Wheatsheaf Book, 1983), 4.
37 Hans J. Morgenthau, *Politics among Nations: The Struggle for Power and Peace*, 5th rev. ed. (New York: Alfred A. Knopf, 1973), 489.
38 Michael H. Louw, *National Security* (Pretoria: University of Pretoria, 1978), ix.
39 James Barros, ed., *The United Nations: Past, Present, and Future* (New York: Free Press, 1972), 17.
40 Johnn E. Mroz, *Beyond Security: Private Perceptions among Arabs and Israelis* (New York: International Peace Academy, 1980), 105.
41 Javeed Ahmed Sheikh, "Security Perception of Weak Nations: A Case Study of Pakistan," in *Security for the Weak Nations*, ed. Syed Farooq Hasnat and Anton Palinka (Lahore: IZHARSONS, 1986), 84.
42 Emma Rothschild, "What is Security," *Daedalus* 24, no. 3 (Summer 1995): 61.
43 Ibid.
44 Muchkund Dubey, "Culture of Peace in Central South Asia," in *Proceedings of UNESCO Sub-Regional Workshop on The Culture of Peace in Central South Asia, Rawalpindi, November 20–22, 1995*, Organized by Foundation for Research on International Environment, National Development and Security (FRIENDS) (Islamabad: Margalla Press, 1995), 63.
45 Barry R. Posen, "The Security Dilemma and Ethnic Conflict," *Survival: Global Politics and Strategy* 35 (1993): 27–47.
46 See Omario Kanji, "Security," in *Beyond Intractability*, ed. G. Burgess and H. Burgess (Conflict Research Consortium, University of Colorado, 2013), http://www.beyondintractability.org/essay/security (accessed December 24, 2013).
47 Niklas L.P. Swantron and Mikael S. Wiessmann, "Conflict, Conflict Prevention, Conflict Management, and Beyond a Conceptual Exploration" (concept paper published by the Central Asia-Caucasus Institute & Silk Road Studies Program, Sweden, 2005), 7.
48 Moonis Ahmer, ed., *Conflict Resolution Research in South Asia* (Karachi: Department of International Relations, University of Karachi, 2010), 19.
49 James A. Schellenberg. *Conflict Resolution: Theory, Research and Practice* (New York: State University of New York Press, 1996), 8.
50 Peter Wallenstein, *Understanding Conflict Resolution*, 3rd ed. (London: SAGE Publications, 2012), 17.
51 Bernard Brodie, "Nuclear Weapons: Strategic or Tactical," *Foreign Affairs*, January 1954.
52 Bernard Brodie, *The Atomic Bomb and American Security*. Occasional Paper no. 18 (Yale Institute of International Studies, 1945).
53 Kenneth N. Waltz, "Nuclear Myths and Political Realities," *The American Political Science Review* 84, no. 3 (September 1990): 731–745.
54 Henry Kissinger, *Nuclear Weapons and Foreign Policy* (New York: Harper and Brothers, 1957).
55 Therese Delpech, *Nuclear Deterrence in the 21$^{st}$ Century* (Santa Monica: RAND Corporation, 2012).
56 Lawrence Freedman, *Deterrence* (Cambridge: Polity Press, 2004), 116.

57 Ward Wilson, "The Myth of Nuclear Deterrence," *Nonproliferation Review* 15, no. 3 (November 2008).
58 See Kenneth Waltz, *Theory of International Politics* (New York: McGraw Hill, 1979).
59 See A.F.K. Organski and Jacek Kugler, *The War Ledger* (Chicago: University of Chicago Press, 1980).
60 Arvind Kumar, "Theories of Deterrence and Nuclear Deterrence in the Subcontinent," in *The India-Pakistan Nuclear Relationship: Theories of Deterrence and International Relations*, ed. E. Sridharam (New Delhi: Routledge 2007), 241.
61 Ibid., 243.
62 David J. Karl, "Proliferation Optimism and Pessimism Revisited," *Journal of Strategic Studies* 34, no. 4 (August 2011): 619–641.
63 See Edited extract from *Post-Cold War Conflict Deterrence* (Naval Studies Board, National Research Council, National Academy of Sciences, 1997), http://www.nap.edu/openbook.php?record_id=5464&page=R5 (accessed October 23, 2014).
64 Ibid.
65 Edward Lock, *Strategic Culture Theory: What, Why and How? September 2017* (Oxford, 1990), 121, https://doi.org/10.1093/acrefore/9780190228637.013.320 (accessed February 5, 2024).

## · 2 ·
# ANALYTICAL TOOLS AND MODELS

## Introduction

To maintain the originality and objectivity of the argument that the deployment of democracy and deterrence in a hybrid manner can serve to attain, maintain, and sustain peace, stability, and security in the region and beyond, it is necessary to assess and evaluate the two subjects on different academic tools and models. For this purpose, several academic models will be deployed that are developed by this author either for earlier research or for this study. These academic tools will help the researchers to deploy in other similar studies as well. However, it is necessary to mention that these models can either be deployed independently or in a hybrid manner to evaluate the argument. Moreover, to ensure logical outcomes from these models, the researchers must suggest improvements in these academic models so they can find a place in the literature.

## Possibility-Probability (P2) Model[1]

This author developed this model for an earlier study as referred, however, it is deployed here again to test the argument related to the efficacy of diplomacy and deterrence in attaining, maintaining, and sustaining peace, stability, and security at all levels.

While developing the P2 model (Figure 1), the theories of possibility and probability were studied. Briefly explaining the two theories, the "possibility theory is an uncertainty theory devoted to the handling of incomplete information,[2] whereas, probability deals with "physical observations associated with games of chance."[3] However, mathematical calculations have been deliberately omitted and only the literal meanings have been considered. For instance, probability would imply, "the relative possibility that an event will occur,"[4] and possibility would reflect that, "may or can be, exist, happen, be done, be used."[5]

For this research, the possibility of a certain event happening between the two states has been taken as "can be," if the leadership considers whether it is desirable, preferable, or favorable, and has the political will to do it. All these elements fall in the domain of intangible elements and cannot be measured mathematically. However, the probability has been considered based on tangible elements related to doability based on capability, capacity, sustainability, and exit strategy.

The scale at which the possibility is evaluated includes doability, desirability, preferability, and favorability. The doability is determined at C7 to see the strengths and weaknesses of the state. The same can be determined

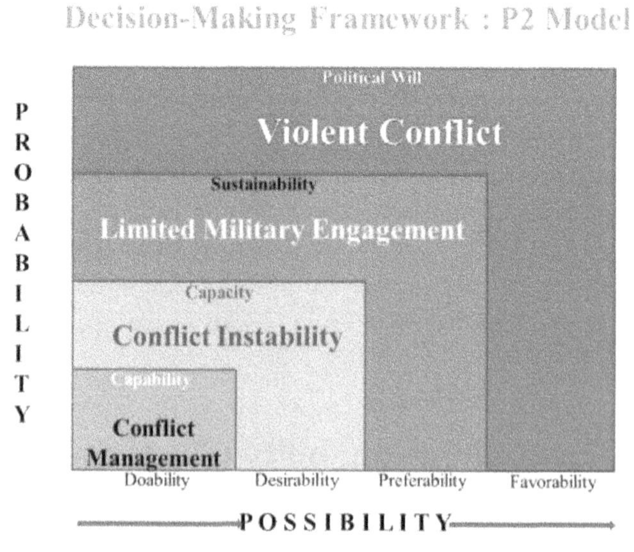

Figure 1. P2 Model.

for the opponent to decide before an offensive is planned. Likewise, the desirability factor reflects the behavior of the decision-makers as what makes them determine that a particular action will be desirable for the state. Similarly, the preferability can only be determined after the geopolitical environment and the national interest of the state that is likely to decide in favor of an offensive action. Lastly, the leadership must understand and evaluate if its actions will gain approval from the regional and international stakeholders.

To understand the complexities of the wars and conflicts between UMPs, the study deployed the P2 Model, to determine the motives and behavior of the initiator, whereas D2 was deployed to understand the response of the defender on selected wars and conflicts of the near past. Following both inductive and deductive methods of reasoning, the dynamic model (P2) helped conclude that the relatively stronger states remain committed to the precepts of realism which is based on power and security to further their interests disregarding even the basic rights to relatively small and weaker states in the developing world.

The prevalent and evolving environment (domestic, regional, and international), leadership at major capitals and the states in conflict, and any other factor that may overcome the existing mechanism such as natural calamities of extraordinary magnitude or extremely violent uprisings in the disputed areas, will also be considered to determine the probabilities of conflicts and wars.

## Diplomacy and Deterrence (D2) Model

The P2 Model can serve as an evaluation and appraisal tool for scenario planning and decision-making from the viewpoint of the attacker on either side. Subsequently, the D2 Model can set the tone of the response by the defenders. The D2 deploys all avenues of diplomacy and deterrence to avert and avoid war through positive diplomacy and aggressive posturing to keep the adversary at bay (Figure 2). However, D2 can be deployed to convince the non-compliant states through coercion, compellence, economic sanctions, isolations, socioeconomic boycotts, and even cancellation of organizational memberships in extreme cases.

On the diplomatic front, the defender activates its alliance partners which can influence the attackers in a significant way. Concurrently, the defender launches an aggressive diplomatic campaign to garner support within the region and beyond. The defender deploys an aggressive media campaign to project itself as innocent and the adversary as the perpetrators of violence.

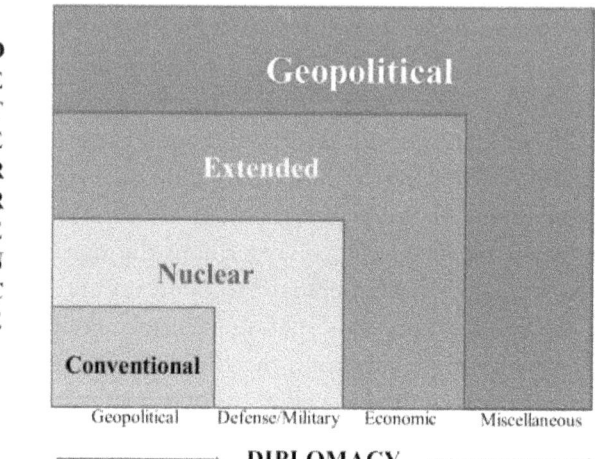

Figure 2. D2 Model.

Since effective diplomacy heavily relies on a state's geographical location and its relevance to world order, therefore, the states must make use of this inherent advantage due to its location that cannot be changed but exploited to its full potential. Some states are isolated due to their geographical locations and cannot play a worthwhile role in geopolitics but have developed themselves in a manner that they are regarded as geo-economic and socio-cultural power centers. For instance, New Zealand is remotely located but appears as a top-ranked country on all the necessary Human Development Indices (HDIs). Likewise, Switzerland's deterrent value lies in its peaceful outlook without any military strength. On the other hand, North Korea and Afghanistan, despite being strategically located do not enjoy a worthwhile diplomatic stature due to their irresponsible behavior toward human rights, freedom of speech, expression, media, and women empowerment.

D2 Model will help the researchers and the practitioners to evaluate a state's response to any aggression against it through its diplomatic approaches and posturing if it has a matching military capability. However, the same will not be seen in the case of wars and conflicts between the UMPs, but diplomatic applications may still bring some relief for the smaller and relatively weaker states.

For instance, if North Korea thrives on its deterrent value due to its nuclear capability, Qatar rides on the diplomatic stature it has earned due to its responsible behavior as a peacemaker in the region. However, all states are not equal in size, natural resources, population, economic prowess, and military strength and may not have a worthwhile deterrent value, therefore it is necessary to form strategic alliances to ensure their existence is not challenged by regional or extra-regional powerhouses. For this purpose, both diplomacy and deterrence must be deployed in a hybrid manner either sequentially or concurrently to achieve the desired national interests.

## C7 Model

To determine the deterrent value of any state, either from the attacker's position or the defender's position, this author has developed an analytical tool, referred to as C7 Model. This academic model can help the researchers understand and evaluate the strengths and weaknesses of any state. Subsequently, this evaluation of the deterrent value can be deployed on the P2 Model for the attacker to decide whether its plans are doable or not, and if these plans would receive worldwide favorability or not. Likewise, the practitioners and strategists can deploy the relevant information to make a considered opinion and make decisions in the best national interests.

The C7 Model can be used to determine the deterrent value either for a single avenue of deterrence or in combination with the defined avenues of deterrence, discussed in detail in Chapter 5. A brief description of each element of the C7 Model is appended below.

First "C" stands for the *Capability* that any state has acquired to further its politico-military objectives. Generally, the capability, a combination of ability and intent, is referred to as military capability, however, this author thinks that it should reflect the total sum of any state's strengths that supports its national interests. Moreover, the capability, if considered in the military domain alone, must be evaluated in both: offensive and defensive.

However, the state's abilities are usually determined based on military strengths according to line comparison of the hardware on the inventory. This process needs a careful analysis of the entire inventory of all three services and the offensive capabilities held by strategic units. This process takes its inspiration from the Chinese sage Sun Tzu's dicta "know your enemy and know yourself in a hundred battles you will never be in peril. When you are ignorant of the enemy but know yourself, your chances of winning or losing are equal. If ignorant both of your enemy and of yourself, you are certain in every battle to be in peril."[6] However, the most important aspect of this exercise is to identify the areas that need careful analysis. Clausewitz has added to Sun Tzu's dicta that "knowing oneself and one's enemy requires at the national strategy, national military, and operational levels."[7]

Second "C" stands for the *Credibility of States*. The credibility of any state to proceed with its planned operations depends on each domain, like leadership (practicality), and equipment (technical). Perhaps, this aspect falls both in the fields of tangible and intangible evaluation. To ensure that a particular state is seriously taken by friendly nations and opponents, a state's behavior must be consistent with its domestic and international commitments both during peacetime and crises.

The states that are dependent on the acquisition of military hardware often lack credibility in their application and execution of operational plans. For deterrence to be effective, it must be based on credible resources in all domains: hardware and leadership's intent.

Third "C" stands for the *Capacity* that any state has as part of its potential war stamina. The aspects related to the capacity of the state include the absorption, execution, and response to any challenges that the state may face. This is extremely important for deterrence including conventional deterrence to hold its ground. The capacity may include a host of factors, but perhaps, the evaluation of the state's deterrent capability may also include, the endurance of its military capability, technological support before and after the envisaged operations, the economic capacity of the state to resist or execute certain operations, and perhaps the country's politico-intellectual capacity to face off the international pressure if against and shore up the diplomatic support if required in favor. The state's capacity not only reflects its appetite to fight for its survival but to expand its area of influence as well. The capacity of the state in the militaristic domain also considers the strategic culture of the society. For instance, Afghan society has proved to be resilient and resistant to foreign occupation since ancient times, however, the Indian sub-continent did not show any resistance to outsiders during its age-old civilization.

Fourth "C" stands for *Communicability by the States*. The communication ability or the communicability of the state's leadership has always been important to strengthen the credibility of the state. However, in contemporary times, it has further gained ground due to evolved methods of communication tools. Its skillful communication by the leadership or other top officials of the state adds value to the state's credibility. Such communication must reflect the intention of the state with clarity, and conciseness.

In today's media-savvy environment where social media has assumed the role of a communicator on behalf of the state, strategic communication is done through narrative building. The communication strategy must be integrated into all strategic, operational, and tactical plans to be effective, and it must be synchronized with the launching of an offensive as well as a defensive campaign.

Fifth "C" stands for *Command Structure of the Armed Forces of the State*. The command structure of each state reflects the strategic culture of the society and represents how it views its security architecture to guarantee the territorial integrity and sovereignty of the state. Most of the democratic states have similar command structures and are organized traditionally. For instance, nearly every state, unless it is landlocked, has an army, navy, and air force to face security challenges. However, to counter evolving threats in the domain of space, a few advanced states have already formed space commands, and some have renamed their air forces as the aerospace force. Likewise, to deal with the evolving hybrid threats posed by the Non-State Actors (NSAs) and the proxies, states have formulated counterterrorism (CT) strategies and commands equipped with Unmanned Combat Aerial Vehicles (UCAVs), either independently or under a traditional structure.

Sixth "C" stands for the *Control of the Security Apparatus*. This relates to the question of who holds the buttons. In most democratic states, civilian elected governments have control of the security apparatus and decide their deployment and employment with the prior approval of the parliament. There is no dispute or discontent in the mechanism and the civilian elected government has full authority to appoint or remove the military leadership on all tiers. However, there are a few states that have a different security architecture. For instance, the military junta is all-powerful in Myanmar and North Korea. Likewise, the development and deployment of nuclear and missile forces is carried out and controlled by the Pakistan Army which has jealously guarded this control over the past five decades and played a central in what Pakistan has today to deter its five-times bigger and larger armed forces of India.

Lastly, perhaps the *Conduct of the States*. Under this broad heading, states are to be evaluated for their behavior internally and externally. The conduct of the states is usually reflective of their historical past, societal norms, social and cultural makeup, internal political structure, and the type of government. The opponents will be keenly studying the governance system of the state, defense spending, peoples' well-being, academic pursuits by the youth including research-related capability and effort by state institutions, and the economic independence or otherwise of the state. Moreover, the state's conduct at relevant forums both internationally, regionally, and internally will be evaluated keenly by the adversaries. Most importantly, states rational and responsible behavior toward international obligations would reflect their future course of action.

## Conclusion

The analytical tools and models (P2, D2, and C7) explained in this chapter will be deployed in subsequent chapters with examples to validate the author's argument that diplomacy and deterrence have to work in a hybrid manner to attain, maintain, and sustain peace, stability, and security in the region and beyond. These models can help researchers and practitioners alike because they are simple and act as the starting point for a comprehensive data analysis.

The C7 Model will help in determining the strengths and weaknesses of any state and with any perspective: attacker or the defender. The collected information will help in scenario planning as well as decision-making processes.

Therefore, the correct sequence in which these assessment tools and analytical models can be deployed is C7 to determine the strengths and weaknesses of oneself and the enemy as the Chinese sage Sun Tzu had directed some 2,500 years ago. "Know yourself and know your enemy."[8] Once the relevant information is available, it should be tested on the P2 Model to evaluate its doability from the attacker's perspective as well as the defender's perspective. However, if the attackers have decided to go ahead with their plans, then the D2 Model can be put into action to evaluate the defender's response in the domain of diplomacy and deterrence.

It is argued that the response will be more effective if diplomacy and deterrence are employed in a hybrid manner and in synch with each other in all situations of the war and conflict: before initiation, during the crisis, and after the events are concluded.

The strengths of these analytical tools lie in their deployment in different situations and on different case studies. These tools and models can be deployed independently as well as in combination to reach a conclusion and draw pertinent lessons. However, this author opines that these models are debated by researchers to determine their efficacy for the purpose they are developed and proposed and suggest measures to improve them to avoid getting false results.

## Notes

1  Zia Ul Haque Shamsi, *Nuclear Deterrence and Conflict Management between India and Pakistan* (New York: Peter Lang, 2020)155
2  Didier Dubois and Henri Prade, *Possibility Theory and Its Applications: Where Do We Stand?* (Toulouse: University of Paul Sabatier, 2011), 1.
3  Robert B. Ash, *Basic Probability Theory* (Mineola, NY: Dover, 1970), 1.
4  http://dictionary.reference.com/browse/probability?s=t (accessed December 14, 2014).
5  http://dictionary.reference.com/browse/possible (accessed December 14, 2014).
6  Defense Technical Information Centre, https://apps.dtic.mil/sti/citations/ADA440962 (accessed February 18, 2024).
7  Ibid.
8  See James Clavell, Sun Tzu's *The Art of War* (Lahore: Combine Printers, 1983).

## · 3 ·
# AVENUES OF DIPLOMACY

## Introduction

Diplomacy remains the most ancient method of approaching and maintaining a working relationship between any two or multiple political entities. It is through prudent diplomacy that the relatively smaller powers survived against the mighty empires in ancient times. Nothing has changed in the international system except that global leaders have been handed over the legitimacy of their acts by the international institutions that they have crafted themselves to justify their doing.

In contemporary times too, the stronger states rely more on the hard power to persuade the opponent whereas the smaller powers depend on the skillful deployment of diplomacy. However, the success lies in the hybrid employment of diplomacy and deterrence to attain, maintain, and sustain peace, stability, and security in the region and beyond.

The beauty of diplomacy lies in its hybrid mannerism as it works relentlessly for war avoidance, but at the same time works tirelessly for planning an impending war to ensure territorial integrity and sovereignty. Moreover, diplomacy is perhaps the most effective tool that any state has to promote and protect its interests. Interestingly, diplomacy has an unchallenged role in all the domains of a sovereign state. Therefore, this chapter is aimed at venturing into the avenues of diplomacy to determine its significance and efficacies in attaining, maintaining, and sustaining global peace, stability, and security.

There is little doubt that every state demands a miraculous outcome from this amazing tool, but it has certain inherent limitations. Diplomacy alone cannot decide the fate of the state. It needs the unwavering support of the leadership and the people of the state. Diplomacy does not operate in a vacuum but on sound logic. To achieve difficult objectives, it takes difficult decisions. Diplomacy must not fear the outcome of its efforts because it can make the opponent think positively. Since diplomacy works in all situations even if the deterrence has failed, the states must opt for a diplomatic solution to any of their conflicts or disagreements with other states.

Diplomacy is at its best when employed offensively. It's not a given tool but needs to be acquired through training, skill development, capacity building, and capability acquisition. Diplomacy acts as a first frontier for any state, in every domain, because it has been practiced by all the previous societies, "as a system of structured communication between two or more parties."[1] Diplomacy teaches forbearance, openness, and accommodation for ideas from all schools of thought. Diplomacy integrates different cultures, religions, and societies in a manner best suited for the state.

## Geo-diplomacy

Diplomacy based on geographical location is perhaps one of the most ancient avenues of building relations with other entities in the region and beyond. Since the geographical location of the states is permanent, the boundaries also remain largely unchanged, meaning that the neighbors cannot be changed. Therefore, the most effective way to achieve peace, stability, and security is to develop cordial relations with immediate neighbors. However, this remains highly contentious because most countries have some territorial disputes with their immediate neighbors, thus entering a protracted conflict if the same is not resolved in the embryonic stage.

However, an ancient philosopher from the Indus Valley civilization Chanakya Kautilya is often quoted as "Your neighbor is your natural enemy and the neighbor's neighbor is your friend."[2] Therefore, the conflict is natural between the two neighbors, and it becomes worse when the states follow Chanakya's dicta of making friends with neighbor's neighbors. For instance, India has good relations with its arch-rival nuclear neighbor Pakistan's immediate neighbors, Afghanistan and Iran. India has been conducting hybrid warfare on Pakistan from these two states that have led to numerous skirmishes with its immediate neighbors along with some serious allegations of proxies operating from these places. Likewise, several countries in the Middle East have disputes with neighboring states which came into being at the end of the formal colonial era. These include disputes between Lebanon and Syria, Iran and the United Arab Emirates (UAE), Turkey and Syria, Israel and Syria, Israel and Lebanon, and many more. Some of these disputes are active and lead to military engagements at regular intervals while some of the dormant conflicts go through the management processes.

On the other hand, geo-diplomacy does not only represent conflicts but also bilateral relations for the promotion of trade, commerce, tourism, and regional stability. For instance, landlocked countries rely heavily on diplomacy to ensure the smooth inflow of goods and services through their neighboring states. Afghanistan's economy is heavily reliant on Pakistan's trade passage to the Arabian Seaports despite protracted territorial claims by the latter.

## External Relations (Primary and Foremost)

Foreign policy of any state aims to further its national interests and the tool that is needed to accomplish this task is diplomacy. The interchangeable use of the two terminologies, at times, creates doubts about the supremacy of one over the other. It is necessary to understand that the first and the foremost task of diplomacy is to promote own state's point of view externally, in the most effective way possible. The point of view that is crafted by the foreign policy of the state is in synch with the national interests of the state. Diplomacy is the art and science of deploying the strengths of national power to achieve national interests, aims, and objectives. Since all states are not equal in size, population, natural resources, and total sum of national power, therefore, it is incumbent upon states to exploit their diplomatic skills to earn the maximum benefits they can.

Winning an argument through diplomatic overtures makes diplomacy look like the most beneficial tool any state has. Diplomacy makes inroads in bilateral relations as well as multilateral relations. Since diplomacy involves multiple nations and cultures, and clashes with diverse interests, therefore, it needs a variety of attributes: patience, persistence, prudence, and productivity (P4). Diplomacy at the bilateral state level adopts an entirely different approach than at the multilateral level. Bilaterally, diplomacy aims to maximize gains vis a vis the other state, whereas multilaterally, a lot of compromises must be made to achieve the objectives.

While diplomacy in its major avenues will be discussed in detail in the following paragraphs, it is necessary to reiterate that diplomacy itself is not what foreign policy of any state is, but it is the most effective tool to accomplish the policy objectives that are crafted to ensure that state's national interest is supreme.

Diplomacy is an offensive tool to further one's interests, whereas deterrence can act as a counteroffensive tool, should diplomacy fail. However, even if the deterrence fails, it keeps the room open for diplomacy to regain intra-war deterrence. Remember, if one has a capability, one would like to test it, deploy it, or even employ it, and if one has a weapon, one will be tempted to use it to see its impact and outcome. Therefore, it is incumbent upon diplomacy not to give up on its efforts for attaining, maintaining, and sustaining peace, stability, and security, under any circumstances.

## Economic Diplomacy

Alongside maintaining and sustaining external relations, perhaps diplomacy works tirelessly to bring economic benefits to the state. Commonly referred to as economic diplomacy, each state attempts to maximize its economic gains either in bilateral relations or through multilateral forums.

Economic diplomacy not only makes gains for a country's economy but also strives to achieve political and security objectives. Soon after the WW II, when Europe had been nearly destroyed, the US offered a Marshall Plan that was aimed at rebuilding Western Europe. The objective was to rebuild the destroyed infrastructure and keep the West European nations under its influence so that they would not incline toward the erstwhile Soviet Union that was controlling the East European states expanding its communist agenda. This was done under the Economic Recovery Act of 1948 and was usually referred to by the US Secretary of State at the time, George Marshall.[3]

Likewise, Pakistan was offered to become a member of the Southeast Asia Treaty Organization (SEATO), primarily due to the strategic location of erstwhile East Pakistan "to prevent communism from gaining ground in the region."[4] Under this fold, a significant amount of financial and military assistance was provided to Pakistan to keep it away from falling into the Soviet camp.

In recent times, China has been playing the cards of economic diplomacy with amazing gains. President Xi Jinping's Belt and Road Initiative (BRI), also referred to as the New Silk Road, is part of China's grand economic diplomacy to gain political and security objectives. Launched in 2013, the project has expanded its wings to Africa, Oceania, and Latin America. One of the flagship projects of BRI runs through the entire length of Pakistan. Titled as China-Pakistan Economic Corridor (CPEC) is aimed at linking the relatively less developed western regions to Pakistan's warm water's deep-sea port of Gwadar, which sits very near the mouth of the Persian Gulf. CPEC is making a significant contribution to Pakistan's much-needed infrastructural development. China has through this plan further strengthened its strategic ties with Pakistan, much to the disappointment of the US.

China's economic diplomacy has raised its political stature manifolds, and the country now leads the Global South whose membership has reached 132 comprised of developing countries across the globe. The success of China's economic diplomacy lies in its sincerity of purpose. China supports developing countries in building critical infrastructure like ports, roads, bridges, energy projects, climate-friendly green projects, and basic amenities projects for education, health, and cultural centers.

## (Defense) Military Diplomacy

"Defense diplomacy, also known as military diplomacy, is the non-violent use of military forces, adapting public diplomacy, through activities like officer exchanges, combined training programs, cultural exchanges, and ship visits, etc., to further a country's diplomatic ties and promoting its international agenda."[5] However, for this research, this author will use military diplomacy.

Military diplomacy as a tool to leverage military objectives is as old as diplomacy and warfare itself. In contemporary times, its significance has grown manifolds, primarily due to evolving alliance formations and increased number of wars and conflicts. Military diplomacy not only serves to achieve bilateral military support to meet any contingencies but also helps in furthering the country's politico-military objectives at multilateral military alliances.

Military diplomacy plays an important and active role in UN Peacekeeping Missions in conflict-ridden regions. It "helps countries navigate the difficult path from conflict to peace. We have unique strengths, including legitimacy, burden sharing, and an ability to deploy troops and police from around the world, integrating them with civilian peacekeepers, to address a range of mandates set by the UN Security Council and General Assembly."[6]

Perhaps the US military diplomatically uses its muscles to further its national interests. "The U.S. military has been a key player in, for instance, the spread of democracy, building partner countries' strength through military-to-military relationships …, personnel exchange, and humanitarian assistance operations."[7] In South Asia also, Pakistan uses its military for the entire gambit of diplomacy: geopolitical, geostrategic, and even geo-economics. "Military diplomacy has helped Pakistan to enhance and strengthen bilateral and multilateral relations with various nations. Joint military exercises, competitions, and troops' contributions to global peace have augmented Pakistan's image as a responsible country."[8] It is necessary to mention that Pakistan has contributed to UN peacekeeping missions whenever and wherever called upon, and the same has been recognized by the world body as well.

Military diplomacy, as part of the main diplomatic effort, plays an important role in furthering the country's politico-military objectives. It acts as a frontline defense in major capitals and alliance headquarters. It also acts as a bridge in averting crises through proactive engagement with its counterparts. Another role that military diplomacy plays is the participation in joint international military exercises, either bilaterally or on a bigger scale. It greatly helps the participating nations develop an understanding of each other's strategic culture, operability of equipment, and the military language that is used by each service. The coordination for planning such mega-level exercises helps nations synergize their strategies to achieve common objectives. For instance, the anti-piracy exercises carried out by the regional and extra-regional navies in the Gulf and Red Sea have been a great help in countering piracy in the areas around the Horn of Africa. One such exercise codenamed *Aman* is a multinational naval Exercise. This exercise is conducted by the Pakistan Navy in which several friendly navies around the world participate and it "includes operations related to anti-piracy, joint maneuverings, rescue operations, naval drills, etc. The Exercise helps participating navies to exchange their experience and knowledge and provides a platform for the participants to nurture their maritime capabilities."[9]

Likewise, the navies of China and Russia "conducted joint anti-piracy drills in the northern part of the Arabian Sea to enhance the capabilities of the two countries militaries in safeguarding strategic maritime routes."[10] For the same purpose, Combined Maritime Forces (CMF) was established in which Navies from 39 nations participate in different exercises regularly. For instance, the Combined Task Force (CTF) 151 is a part of CMF, and its mission is "to take actions, within its area of operations, to directly suppress piracy outside territorial waters of Coastal States."[11]

Military diplomacy also helps in organizing International Defence Expos and showcasing of own country's defense production capabilities. This plays an important role in promoting defense exports and provides opportunities to view and analyze the displayed equipment of other nations. Moreover, high-level interactions take place that help in networking the military officials at different levels. Each developed and developing country showcases its best produce on such forums, both military and non-military, or the dual-use emerging technologies to earn orders to grow its business. These expos serve as one-window operations for the acquisition of arms and equipment and help the acquiring nations to carry out a comparative analysis of the desired equipment, which is otherwise a very tedious process.

Military diplomacy also targets the *Defence Universities and Colleges* across the globe to get the country's manpower trained in the renowned states particularly the officers with promising careers. For instance, the National Defense University (NDU) of the US, Pakistan, Royal College of Defense Services (RCDS), UK, Australian Defence College, Australia, etc., are well-known institutions for training military and civilian officials on policy, strategy, and doctrine. Consequently, these defense institutions act as marketing tools because they offer customized courses to students of allied and friendly countries. The curriculum includes exhaustive lessons on the historical development of the host country, its culture, and its strengths. The graduating officers, no matter where they come from, do carry home an imprint of the host country and it is commonly stated that the students would act as *Ambassadors* for the country they have been trained in.

The most interesting aspect of military diplomacy lies in its hybrid character. A military diplomat works relentlessly to avoid wars and conflicts, and at the same time spends a lot of time planning for the next war with the allies. Today, nearly every state has its military attaches in major diplomatic missions across the globe. These officers not only report back on military build-ups in the country of deployment but also keep a watch on regional developments through their contacts with other diplomats. This is a typical role of a military diplomat in that he/she may be involved in both positive and negative diplomacy. Perhaps this is one reason why military diplomats around the world are kept under strict watch by the host countries.

One must refer to the highly skilled display of military diplomacy by Qatar during the period of blockade by the neighborly Gulf nations. Qatar successfully activated all avenues of military diplomacy: activation of strategic relations with Turkey to the maintenance of strategic partnership with the US, to avert an impending physical assault on the tiny peninsular Gulf state by a formidable alliance at the time in June 2017. Qatar made the best use of its military diplomacy and invited Turkish armed forces for the military exercises soon after the blockade was announced by the KSA-led quartet and used the presence of the US forces in the Al Udeid Air Base on its soil. "Qatar is a good friend and reliable and capable partner. I'm notifying Congress that I will designate Qatar as a major non-NATO ally to reflect the importance of our relationship. I think it's long overdue,"[12] President Biden told reporters with the Emir of Qatar sitting at his side.

## Religious/Ideological Diplomacy

Diplomacy in any domain aims to further the interests of any country and there is no avenue where the religious ideology does not figure out prominently. Sometimes referred to as ideological diplomacy, this author thinks that the introduction of Abrahamic religions has played an important role in geopolitics ever since and therefore must be discussed through the lens of diplomacy.

Religion as a driver of change has been a very strong motivator for the people that one can risk his/her life to promote and protect. One needs to investigate the history of religious expansion. Initial messages of invitation to join a particular religion were always through the messengers, now referred to as diplomats. The Prophet Muhammad (PBUH) sent his representatives to different nearby and distant states and empires of the time, inviting them to join Islam. Well-worded letters were sent to Egyptian ruler Al-Muqawqis in the sixth year of Hijri and to Emperor Ashama ibn Abjar in Ethiopia, Heraclius, the emperor of the Byzantine Empire, Chosroes, the king of Persia, Munzir ibn Sawa, the ruler of Bahrain, Himyarite Harith, the prince of Yemen, and Harith Gassani, the governor of Sham.[13] These letters and messages proved extremely useful in convincing people to join the new religion, except in a few places like Persia.

Likewise, religious diplomacy was used in making alliances between different tribes well before the Treaty of Westphalia gave the concepts of states. This strategy was adopted by all the major religions in the early years of the expansion of Islam and later on during the Crusades. The process continued during the Ottoman Empire's expansion as well as its decline.

Another important avenue that diplomacy deals with religious issues is the intolerance in Western societies for the Holy Books of Islam and the Prophet Muhammad (PBUH). Quite often, the incident of desecration of the Al-Quran happens in the developed West, and the disrespect of the Holy Prophet (PBUH) is shown under the garb of freedom of expression. Such incidents immediately raise the level of anger across the Muslim world and lead to unrest in some places. Although the UN has declared March 15, 2023, as a day to tackle Islamophobia, there is no respite from such incidents.

Likewise, religiously motivated philanthropy is also an avenue that many countries use as diplomatic missions. India has built one of the largest Hindu temples in UAE, which was inconceivable until PM Modi's religious diplomacy succeeded in convincing the Islamic state's ruler that it is needed for the Indian population residing in the Emirates. Likewise, the Saudi government has opened its Holy Sites of Madinah to the official delegations from different countries and different religions which was inconceivable until the beginning of this century.[14]

Qatar successfully showcased its religious ideology at the opening and closing ceremonies of FIFA-2022. All over the country, particularly at the tourism sites, Quranic Verses and Prophet Muhammad's (PBUH) sayings were calligraphed before the mega sporting event rolled out on November 19, 2020, with an impressive opening ceremony at the newly built *Al-Bayt* stadium in Al-Khor, Qatar.

The worldwide organization of ideological rituals is a part of diplomacy where the nations prove themselves as liberals and secular. Indonesia and Malaysia are extremely diverse religious societies but living in peace and harmony since last so many centuries and do project this aspect as part of their ideological tolerance.

India, though has a secular constitution, is failing in this domain under the present BJP regime and has imposed curbs on minorities in the performance of their religious rituals. Moreover, it has built a massive Hindu Temple at the site of a historical Babri Masjid of the Moghul era, further ruining its secular image.

Religious diplomacy plays a central role in promoting religious tourism. Several countries are home to several Holy sites that are visited every year by thousands of pilgrims. For instance, Saudi Arabia is home to Two Holy Mosques that are highly sacred for Muslims, and millions of worshippers visit the country around the year, particularly at the time of the yearly pilgrimage of Hajj. Likewise, Iran and Iraq are home to several sacred sites for Shiite Muslims and receive millions of devotees every year. Similarly, the Vatican City is the seat of the Roman Catholic Church and is visited by nearly five million visitors every year.

There are several Holy Sites for all Abrahamic religions in the Israeli city of Jerusalem including the Temple Mount hosting Al Aqsa Mosque and the Dome of Rock. "This enormous area is also the third most important site to Muslims falling behind only to Mecca and Medina. It is the site where Prophet Muhammad (PBUH) made his ascent to the heavens."[15]

India and Pakistan are home to numerous Holy sites of multiple religions. For instance, India is home to an ancient religion, Hinduism, and holds hundreds of religious sites of the religion practiced by nearly a billion people. India also holds one of the most sacred sites for Sikhism, The Golden Temple, in the city of Amritsar. Likewise, Pakistan is also home to some very important Holy sites of Sikhism: Nankana Sahib, Kartarpur, and a few others in the city of Hasan Abdal and Lahore. Also, Pakistan has important religious sites of some of the ancient religions like Buddhism, and Hinduism, as well. However, the country has failed to exploit the potential of religious diplomacy to build its image enough to receive a greater number of tourists or develop it into a soft power like other nations, mentioned above.

## Public Diplomacy

This is another avenue of diplomacy that greatly helps in building the image and furthering own interests beyond one's frontiers. Also called people's diplomacy, it "includes all official efforts to convince targeted sectors of foreign opinion to support or tolerate a government's strategic objective. Methods include statements by decision-makers, purposeful campaigns conducted by government organizations dedicated to public diplomacy, and efforts to persuade international media to portray official policies favorably to foreign audiences."[16]

The most important objective of public diplomacy is to mild public opinion in favor of one's own state's viewpoint on matters of public interest. The process usually starts with a grapevine and the initial reaction may lead to a formal strategy to achieve the objectives. The method is usually deployed to convince the people to wage a war to secure their interests and get the funding approved.

Likewise, public diplomacy works relentlessly to improve a country's image and soft power. Inviting students from different countries for education and training through scholarships form integral tactics of public diplomacy. Moreover, government-funded Non-Governmental Organizations (NGOs) consistently strive to project their own country's soft power through welfare projects, particularly in the least developed areas.

The US-led Western world vigorously pursues the establishment of democratic values in the countries that have either autocratic rule or monarchies. In the bargain, at times they end up creating conflicts in the society of the target country. The US experience in Afghanistan to promote democracy and women's rights has failed primarily due to societal constraints. Afghan society is primarily tribal and does not subscribe to democracy or women's empowerment. Perhaps the methodology of the US was also not in conformity to public diplomacy in this case, because first the US bombed the country and raised it to the ground looking for 9/11 perpetrators and then tried to install a government of its choice. This was certainly not acceptable to Afghans and therefore after two decades-long occupation, the US had to leave Afghanistan in haste and handed over the reins again to the same Taliban who were not recognized by them throughout these 20 years of occupation.

At other places in the Middle East, public diplomacy by the US does not augur well, primarily due to its blatant support for Israeli atrocities against the Palestinian people. Israeli retaliation to Hamas attacks of October 7, 2023, is outrightly supported by the US and its allies, and despite repeated calls by the people around the world, the US continues to veto the ceasefire resolutions in the UNSC. This act of support to Israel against the people of Palestine in general and Gaza, in particular, had created an extremely adverse impression of the Biden Administration and meant collusion in the Gaza genocide of the children, women, and non-combatants.

Russia also tarnished its image when it launched its ground offensive in Ukraine on February 24, 2022. Barring a few abstentions, many of the countries in the UNGA voted against Russia for its aggression against Ukraine. The entire US-led Western world continues to support Ukraine in its resistance to Russia's offensive in all domains: militarily, financially, and morally, hence Russia loses in the domain of public diplomacy in most of the world.

Contrarily, China has done well in public diplomacy across all continents. Despite all the disinformation and propaganda campaigns by the US-led Western world against China's BRI since its launching in 2013, the project remains highly popular and productive through the lens of public diplomacy.

The plan encompasses a comprehensive development in infrastructure, ports, energy, and projects for people's welfare in the least developed regions and countries.

This author recommended an approach of adopting a nation under the domain of public diplomacy through which the developed nations could help the developing states by appropriating reasonable funds for the public welfare projects in the recipient country. These funds could be exclusively utilized for the provision of basic amenities like education, health, energy, and socioeconomic development of the least developed states to reduce poverty, enhance literacy, improve health indicators, and provision of equal opportunities to all segments of society. Furthermore, to counter any misuse of these funds, the amount could be directly disbursed to the executing authority, co-monitored by the donor state and the host country.

## Cultural Diplomacy[17]

Cultural diplomacy is perhaps one of the most effective tools in promoting the important interests of any state regardless of its military or economic strengths. This has been the practice since ancient times because the conduct of the people projecting their cultural values inspired people of different societies and regions.

According to the Institute of Cultural Diplomacy, "Cultural Diplomacy may best be described as a course of actions, which are based on and utilize the exchange of ideas, values, traditions and other aspects of culture or identity, whether to strengthen relationships, enhance socio-cultural cooperation, promote national interests and beyond; Cultural diplomacy can be practiced by either the public sector, private sector or civil society, either the public sector, private sector or civil society."[18]

For diplomacy to be effective, the socio-cultural domain provides a variety of avenues that are non-existent under any other banner, primarily because it interacts with people directly. Nearly all states make an extra effort to attract people from other states and societies to integrate with their culture which includes the lifestyles of the common people: the food, the clothes, norms and practices, choreography, cinemas, and even the family functions. Therefore, diplomacy is both the art and science of people's interaction with the people of other cultures, and societies.[19] While the primary purpose of diplomacy remains the protection and promotion of the state's interests, the cultural aspect adds value to the image of the state deploying diplomatic efforts in the socio-cultural domains.

Interestingly, cultural diplomacy not only showcases the societal norms and practices of a particular state or region but also plays a significant part in bilateral and multilateral negotiations and agreements. For instance, the Taliban government does not subscribe to the Western viewpoint about women's empowerment and hence remains unrecognized by international organizations and sovereign states. This is primarily due to Afghan culture that is averse to women's empowerment, perhaps due to its practice of being a tribal society.

The states, through the employment of cultural diplomacy, strive to advance their values to other societies. The same was seen during the entire period of colonization when the colonizers promoted their language, cuisine, rituals, and lifestyles, even to some of the very ancient civilizations like India.

Now, India is successfully reversing the process through its Non-Resident Indians (NRIs) across the globe and through its famous film industry of Bollywood. Likewise, mango diplomacy by Pakistan in the US, and Bus Diplomacy by India to lessen the tension between the two nuclear neighbors in South Asia, did prove to be breakers.

The beauty of cultural diplomacy lies in its diversity. While people may feel the difference of regional cultures like that of South Asia and the Middle East even if the two regions are comprised of most Muslim states, they can even taste a difference within the regions like African states which largely differ in tribal cultures of the neighboring states. Likewise, Qatar successfully promoted its culture during FIFA-2022, yet it adopted itself to welcome people from different cultures, regions, and societies. On the other hand, Saudi Arabia which has practiced the Islamic culture since ancient times, has slowly started to show some flexibility for other societies during their visits to the Kingdom. Unfortunately, some Western countries have banned Muslim women from wearing a Hijab that has been part of their dress since the inception of Islam. Moreover, it is against their values of freedom to practice one's values.

However, cultural diplomacy could be more effective if the states designate cultural counselors in each other's diplomatic missions with a specific purpose. It can help promote the soft image of the country and create opportunities to bring the people of the respective state closer by organizing and participating in events of public interest.

## Sports Diplomacy

This is another avenue of diplomacy that attracts the common people beyond borders. Sporting events of any kind, from any state, religion, culture, or background, catch the attention of the people very quickly. Historically, states have used sports as part of diplomatic missions to promote one's image and interests.

Qatar used FIFA-2022 to promote its soft power and claimed a spot as a major sports-loving nation in the region. The successful organization of the event won the hearts of the participants and their supporters alike. The visitors from all countries, regardless of size and standing, were accorded a VIP welcome to the tiny Gulf state. The supporters of each country were provided with flags, caps, shirts, and badges to cheer up their teams on the match day, free of cost. This was unprecedented in FIFA's history. Qatar did earn a lot of goodwill through its acts of hospitality during and after the event.

At times, it does not necessarily mean that a certain state is using sports diplomacy to promote its soft power. It comes all by itself. Today, Messi is a household name across the globe, and hence Argentina automatically becomes a favorite country and gets support without any effort by the state. The same was seen during FIFA-2022 in Qatar, much before Argentina became the world champions.

Likewise, Rafael Nadal for Spain, Novak Djokovic for Serbia, Cristiano Ronaldo for Portugal, and many more sportsmen and women's contributions to their country are without any worthwhile effort of the respective states. However, the flags of the states are proudly hoisted due to individual efforts. Moreover, sports are a healthy activity that attracts people from all walks of life, regardless of caste, creed, color, and affiliations. Yet. it has been repeatedly seen that international sporting events are politicized by nations particularly those against the Western hegemony. For instance, The Olympics have often been an opportunity to enhance peace and dialogue among nations, but like almost everything else, they also fall victim to politicization.

"In 1980, the United States led a boycott of the Summer Olympic Games in Moscow to protest the late 1979 Soviet invasion of Afghanistan. In total, 65 nations refused to participate in the games, whereas 80 countries sent athletes to compete."[20] Likewise, "Washington's recent decision to stage a 'diplomatic boycott' of the 2022 Beijing Winter Olympics is another example of how one of the world's most popular global sporting events has fallen victim to global politics."[21]

Sporting events around the world and the year serve as the perfect diplomatic forums for nations because the athletes represent their states as perfect ambassadors. They not only project a soft image of their states but also act as commercial counselors for their states. The sporting giants at different levels are deployed by respective states to undertake public diplomacy to promote the interest of the state. The celebrity status of the popular athletes helps promote the respective states and at times International Organizations employ them as their representatives to a noble cause. Accordingly, "Sports could be a diplomatic bridge to peace and a vehicle for healing political and cultural rifts among communities, speakers told the General Assembly today as it reviewed progress in implementing its 2012 resolution on the potential of sport to be used as an educational and development tool."[22] Likewise, "United Nations Secretary-General Ban Ki-moon opined that sport is increasingly recognized as an important tool in helping the United Nations achieve its objectives, in particular the Millennium Development Goals. By including sport in development and peace programs more systematically, the United Nations can make full use of this cost-efficient tool to help us create a better world."[23] Nearly all experts and officials of the UN agree that "Sport has a crucial role to play in the efforts of the United Nations to improve the lives of people around the world. Sport builds bridges between individuals and across communities, providing a fertile ground for sowing the seeds of development and peace."[24]

Interestingly, the UN makes good use of sports, sportsmen, and sportswomen across the globe for welfare projects. Every year the UN appoints several sportsmen and sportswomen as its Ambassadors of Goodwill to promote peace, cultures, and humanity across different cultures. For instance, Retired Olympic champion gymnast Li Ning has been named the first Chinese anti-hunger ambassador for the UN World Food Program.[25]

## Regional Diplomacy

Regional diplomacy remains one of the most common methods of forging alliances either to strengthen security or socioeconomic ties. Nearly all regions have formed regional alliances and some of these have proved to be extremely effective and beneficial for the regional states. For instance, the ASEAN is perhaps the most peaceful and integrated regional association despite being extremely diverse in ethnic, religious, and cultural outlook. On the other hand, the SAARC whose membership has a population of nearly two billion remains dormant and one of the most ineffective regional associations around the world. Likewise, the GCC, a sub-regional organization in the Middle East is not only geographically contiguous but also has religious and cultural commonalities. The serious differences in GCC surfaced when three of the member states in concert with an extra-regional player Egypt imposed a blockade on its smaller neighbor, Qatar from June 2017 till December 2020. However, now the situation has returned to normal.

Other regional organizations that provide a platform to make diplomatic advances include the African Union (AU), Asian-African Legal Consultative Organization (AALCO), Arab League (AL), Arab Maghreb Union (AMU), Caribbean Community (CARICOM), Council of Europe (CoE), Community of Latin American and Caribbean States (CELAC), Economic Cooperation Organization (ECO), European Union (EU), Eurasian Economic Union (EAEU), Pacific Alliance (PA), Pacific Islands Forum (PIF), Shanghai Cooperation Organization (SCO), and Southern Common Market (MERCOSUR).[26]

Most of these regional associations are established to expand and enhance the cooperation among the member states in the domain of trade, commerce, tourism, culture, sports, and necessary collaboration to counter the growing menace of extremism and terrorism. The control of proxies and NSAs has been a priority among the regional associations to fight a common enemy. For instance, the EU has developed and deployed a joint strategy to counter terrorism and its fight against hybrid warfare.

However, there are regional organizations that are dormant and have failed in their stated objectives primarily due to wars and conflicts between a few member states. For instance, the SAARC was established on December 8, 1985, with its Secretariat in Kathmandu, Nepal. All South Asian states, Bangladesh, Bhutan, India, the Maldives, Nepal, Pakistan, and Sri Lanka, are its founding members. However, Afghanistan joined the group in April 2007.[27]

Even though the SAARC was established "to promote economic growth, social progress and cultural development within the South Asia region …. Promote the welfare of the peoples … improve their quality of life, accelerate economic growth, social progress, and cultural development,"[28] yet it failed in its objectives due to protracted conflicts between two of its important members: India and Pakistan. Hence, SAARC failed on both accounts: diplomacy and deterrence. While it failed to deter its members from avoiding wars and conflicts, it also failed in its diplomatic efforts to convince them to forge peace, stability, and security in the region.

## International Diplomacy

This form of diplomacy provides several forums to advance a country's national interests. From security to human rights, and refugees to the fight against poverty, hunger, and pandemics, the international forums are open and available to member states. International diplomacy at times may fail in the domain of security issues primarily because of geopolitical compulsions of the leading nations that have veto power. For instance, the US has consistently vetoed the ceasefire resolutions in genocidal acts of Israel, yet the UNSC remains the only forum at which some voices can be raised.

Several regional organizations have now expanded to attain the status of international organizations. For instance, the SCO is an intergovernmental organization founded in Shanghai on June 15, 2001. The SCO currently comprises eight Member States (China, India, Kazakhstan, Kyrgyzstan, Russia, Pakistan, Tajikistan, and Uzbekistan), four Observer States interested in acceding to full membership (Afghanistan, Belarus, Iran, and Mongolia), and six "Dialogue Partners" (Armenia, Azerbaijan, Cambodia, Nepal, Sri Lanka, and Turkey).[29] However, it kept on expanding and in 2021, "the decision was made to start the accession process of Iran to the SCO as a full member, and Egypt, Qatar, as well as Saudi Arabia, became dialogue partners."[30] Now, SCO has attained the status of an international organization with its focus on "regional security issues, its fight against regional terrorism, ethnic separatism and religious extremism."[31]

Likewise, the BRICS started in 2006 as BRIC (Brazil, Russia, India, and China) but became BRICS when South Africa joined the group in 2010. "The group was designed to bring together the world's most important developing countries, to challenge the political and economic power of the wealthier nations of North America and Western Europe."[32] However, with the joining of Egypt, Ethiopia, Iran, Saudi Arabia, and the UAE with effect from 1 January 2024, the organization has attained the status of a powerful international organization which now has its deterrent value in multiple domains.

## Conclusion

The various avenues of diplomacy discussed in this chapter can play a crucial role in attaining, maintaining, and sustaining peace, and stability in any region either independently or in concert with others. Sports connect people of different cultures, communities, and nations. Sports do not recognize state boundaries. It creates healthy competition among the nations and connects the people. Imagine a state that does not have sports at the international level, yet the people love that sport and choose a country to support it even if they are far apart geographically and culturally. For instance, Pakistan's football team does not have a worthwhile standing on FIFA ranking, but the country produces the hardware (footballs) essentially required for the event to take place, and the people of Pakistan feel immensely proud that their product is part of the mega event. Moreover, the people of Pakistan supported Argentina only because Messi was on the field, even if the two nations were far apart on the defined socio-cultural scale.

This author opines that the avenues of diplomacy must be fully deployed while nations strive for peace, stability, and security. The diplomacy must not feel deterred from making efforts in the employment of all these avenues independently or in combination to achieve the stated objectives. The clear manifestation of the same was seen during the blockade of Qatar during 2017–2020. The small peninsular state left no stone unturned to achieve peace and stability in the region by averting a near-war situation through bold diplomacy alone because its armed forces could hardly serve as a deterrent against a much larger regional coalition that had initiated the blockade.

This author thinks that the states must adopt the mechanism of productive engagement by deploying a variety of diplomatic avenues to achieve peace and stability across all regions. Therefore, it is incumbent upon the world leaders to deploy all available diplomatic means in every possible domain: technology, trade, and tourism, to enhance the probability of attaining, and sustaining peace and stability at the regional level and then expanding it to the global level.

## Notes

1 Stephen McGlinchey, "Diplomacy," *E-International Relations*, January 2017, https://www.e-ir.info/2017/01/08/diplomacy/ (accessed July 18, 2023).
2 Mir Adnan Aziz, *India: A Prisoner of History*, Part-I, June 11, 2020, https://www.thenews.com.pk/print/670789-india-a-prisoner-of-history-part-i (accessed February 9, 2024).
3 Milestone Documents: Marshall Plan (1948), https://www.archives.gov/milestone-documents/marshall-plan#:~:text=On%20April%203%2C%201948%2C%20President,economic%20infrastructure%20of%20postwar%20Europe (accessed July 20, 2023).
4 Milestones: 1953–1960, https://history.state.gov/milestones/1953-1960/seato#:~:text=In%20September%20of%201954%2C%20the,gaining%20ground%20in%20the%20region (accessed July 20, 2023).

5. A.N.M. Muniruzzaman, "Defence Diplomacy: A Powerful Tool of Statecraft," *CLAWS Journal* 13, no. 2 (2020): 63–80.
6. United Nations Peacekeeping, https://peacekeeping.un.org/en (accessed July 20, 2023).
7. Emi Abitz, *The Use of Military Diplomacy in Great Power Competition: Lessons from the Marshall Plan*, February 12, 2019, https://www.brookings.edu/articles/the-use-of-military-diplomacy-in-great-power-competition/ (accessed January 21, 2024).
8. Omay Aiman, "The Essence of Military Diplomacy," *Pakistan Today*, December 10, 2023.
9. Zara Ahsan, *Issue Brief on "Pakistan's Aman Exercise,"* May 18, 2023, https://issi.org.pk/issue-brief-on-pakistans-aman-exercise/#:~:text='Aman'%20is%20a%20multinational%20naval,operations%2C%20naval%20drills%2C%20etc. (accessed January 21, 2024).
10. China, Russia hold joint anti-piracy drills in Arabian Sea, *Global Times*, January 25, 2022.
11. CTF 151: Counter-piracy, https://combinedmaritimeforces.com/ctf-151-counter-piracy/ (accessed January 21, 2024).
12. Jeff Mason, "Biden Tells Emir He Will Make Qatar a Major Non-NATO ally," *Reuters*, February 1, 2022.
13. https://english.alarabiya.net/features/2017/05/14/In-Pictures-Prophet-Mohammed-s-letters-to-heads-of-states (accessed July 21, 2023).
14. Indian delegation led by Simitri Devi visited Madinah in January 2024.
15. Holy Sites in Jerusalem, https://www.touristisrael.com/holy-sites-in-jerusalem/45601/ (accessed January 21, 2024).
16. https://www.britannica.com/topic/public-diplomacy (accessed July 21, 2023).
17. Some part under this heading was published *Pakistan Journal of Humanities and Social Sciences* 11, no. 4 (2023), while this project was under review.
18. https://www.culturaldiplomacy.org/index.php?en_culturaldiplomacy (accessed July 21, 2023).
19. What Is Diplomacy? https://www.cyber-diplomacy-toolbox.com/Diplomacy.html#:~:text=Diplomacy%20is%20the%20art%2C%20the,relations%2C%20while%20maintaining%20peaceful%20relationships (accessed December 3, 2023).
20. The Olympic Boycott, 1980, https://2001-2009.state.gov/r/pa/ho/time/qfp/104481.htm#:~:text=In%201980%2C%20the%20United%20States,countries%20sent%20athletes%20to%20compete (accessed January 25, 2024).
21. A Brief History of Olympic Boycotts, TRT World, https://www.trtworld.com/magazine/a-brief-history-of-olympic-boycotts-52406 (accessed January 25, 2024).
22. General Assembly Recognizes Value of Sports as Tool for Peace, Development, During Debate Reviewing Resolution's Implementation, Sixty-Ninth Session, 28th Meeting (AM), GA/11572, 20 October 2014.
23. Sports & Development: The UN Perspective on Sports and Development, Sports and Development.org, January 25, 2024.
24. Wilfried Lemke, Special Adviser to the Secretary-General on Sport for Development and Peace, https://www.sportanddev.org/sport-and-development/uns-perspective-sport-and-development (accessed January 25, 2024).
25. Li Ning Named First Chinese Rep to WFP, *CBC News*, October 14, 2009.
26. https://asean.org/our-communities/asean-political-security-community/outward-looking-community/external-relations/international-regional-organisation/ (accessed February 9, 2024).
27. Zia Ul Haque Shamsi, "SAARC Highway," *The Daily Times (Pakistan)*, May 10, 2021.

28 South Asian Association for Regional Cooperation (SAARC), https://www.saarc-sec.org/ (accessed February 21, 2024).
29 Shanghai Cooperation Organization, https://dppa.un.org/en/shanghai-cooperation-organization (accessed February 21, 2024).
30 Ibid.
31 Ibid.
32 "BRICS: What Is the Group and Which Countries Have Joined?" *BBC News*, February 1, 2024, https://www.bbc.com/news/world-66525474 (accessed February 21, 2024).

# · 4 ·
# SIGNIFICANCE OF DIPLOMACY AS A TOOL FOR PEACE, STABILITY, AND SECURITY

## Introduction

Diplomacy works at its best when deployed in synergy with all its attributes and at all available avenues. Diplomacy must not fear the result of failure but aims to win the argument using all available means provided by the state. Diplomacy may have shades of positivity and negativity, but in all forms, it remains dominant over all other ways and means to achieve the political objectives of the state. The role of diplomacy in furthering the state's interests remains supreme and it must not falter in that domain under any circumstances. However, the same holds good for other states too. Diplomacy demands vision, skills, and means to its ways to make it more effective among the comity of nations. The state does not have to have nuclear weapons or large standing armies to either avert a war or win a war, but the unwavering support of its people, and skills with whatever resources the state has. Therefore, if deployed skillfully, diplomacy can do wonders for the relatively smaller states that may not have a strong deterrent value based on the hard power.

Qatar, a small peninsular state in the Gulf was faced with an imminent threat to its existence as a sovereign state on June 5, 2017, when a group of four nations: Saudi Arabia, UAE, Bahrain (all Gulf neighbors), and Egypt, imposed a blockade in all domains: physical land border, aerial borders, ports, economic, social, and diplomatic blockade. The initiators of the unjust and uncalled-for blockade of a much smaller brotherly Muslim country made some 13 demands that included the demands of scaling down the diplomatic relations with Iran and cutting off trade, commerce, and all types of military and intelligence ties by complying with US and international sanctions.[1] Likewise, close the under-construction Turkish military base, and halt military cooperation with Turkey inside of Qatar. The KSA-led quartet further demanded that Qatar must sever ties to all "terrorist, sectarian and ideological organizations," specifically the Muslim Brotherhood, ISIL, al-Qaeda, Fateh al-Sham (formerly known as the Nusra Front) and Lebanon's Hezbollah."[2] One of the most compelling demands was to shut down Al Jazeera and its affiliate stations across the globe. The list went on and included the charges of supporting terror outfits in the region and interfering in the internal affairs of other states. The initiators even demanded hefty reparations for the financial losses caused by the policies.

Qatar managed the crisis that threatened its existence as a political entity by utilizing all available means led by bold diplomacy. At first, Qatar rejected all charges as baseless and called for a negotiated settlement of the conflict in a peaceful manner. Concurrently, Qatar deployed its diplomatic skills in all avenues: economic to social, defense to sports, thereby denying the initiators any niche to exploit and invade the country during the entire period of crisis which lasted over three years. Qatar proved to be a responsible state that was respected for its humanitarian assistance in conflict zones like Gaza, and its facilitation of the dialogue for peace between the US and Afghan Taliban even during the period of blockade. Therefore, Qatar did have goodwill among the comity of nations and hence many of the regional and extraregional states did not support the KSA-led quartet in the blockade. Finally, the initiators gave up and lifted the sanctions in December 2020 without any of their demands met by Qatar at any stage during and after the crisis.

Therefore, the significance of diplomacy as an essential tool to strive for peace, stability, and security, across regions and the globe cannot be overemphasized. However, this author aims to establish that diplomacy if supported by deterrence can be more effective in achieving the task in case of conflicts between the UMPs.

## Diplomacy and Its Nuances

While diplomacy is an essential tool to further the interests of the state, it may have genuine limitations due to the stubbornness of relevant stakeholders. But it must never cease to explore other options. However, diplomacy needs to be complemented by other elements of soft power that must be based on political stability, a robust economy, a tolerant society, and a motivated human resource.

Since the Western world is sensitive to gender discrimination, and rightly so, the states with a poor record of women's education, empowerment, and equality, would not get due respect, no matter how strong the diplomatic maneuvers are. Likewise, if a state has a poor record of human rights, child abuse, and information blackout, it will not be able to impress the other nations that sincerely believe in these concepts.

Great Britain's wartime Prime Minister Winston Churchill's words, though contested for veracity, sum up the art of diplomacy. Churchill had supposedly said, "Diplomacy is the art of telling people to go to hell in such a way that they ask for directions."[3] Diplomacy remains at work even if the leadership is on holidays. It finds ways and develops practical options for the leadership to select a particular course of action so that the state interests are protected and concurrently promoted. The art of diplomacy is to make the opponent feel that the proposal is to their benefit while expanding one's interests. It must project sincerity of purpose and not let an iota of doubt be felt by those sitting across the table.

However, diplomacy may be severely affected due to realpolitik, and the same can be seen in the case of relatively stronger nations' behavior in the domain of international relations. For instance, Israel can get away with its behavior of ignoring calls by international organizations and communities to stop atrocities and genocide of the people of Palestine due to its immense diplomatic leverage over the US and the Western world.

The U.S. Department of State defines diplomacy as "the art and practice of conducting negotiations and maintaining relations between nations; skill in handling affairs without arousing animosity."[4] According to Paul Kreutzer, "the essence of diplomacy is communication between different parties to reach agreement on an issue or a basis for state interaction."[5] Essentially, diplomacy paves the way for the advancement of the state's national interests, and hence it plays the most important role in the international system between states bilaterally or at multilateral forums. Diplomacy is not only the frontline of defense for any state, but an enabler as well to launch an offensive if required. For instance, hectic lobbying takes place for a considerable period before a multilateral Treaty or Agreement is placed for voting at the UN or any such forums.

Diplomacy shapes the perception of the outside world and how it looks at a particular state, perhaps in a similar way as the financial institutions give business suitability ratings for the favorability of investments or otherwise. While diplomacy is not restricted in domains and has a role to play in every aspect, its proclivity is essentially in economy, military, culture, tourism, trade, crisis management, and conflict resolution.

Usually, states go to war for various reasons. The most important often is the failure of diplomacy to manage or resolve disputes; and secondly when deterrence also fails due to lack of will or capability to avert a military engagement. Therefore, it is necessary that at least one should work to avoid wars and conflicts, and the other should endeavor to explore the probabilities of conflict resolutions.

The essentiality of diplomacy as a tool to avert wars and conflicts, and to attain, maintain, and sustain peace, stability, and security cannot be overemphasized. Using bilateral relations, and multilateral forums, diplomacy in concert with other elements of national power, always remains at work to secure peace in the region, and ultimately the globe.

## Positive Diplomacy

While the many avenues of diplomacy are discussed in detail in Chapter 3, its shades: positive and negative, must be deliberated upon here to reiterate its efficacy for peace, stability, and security.

This author defines positive diplomacy as an effort by states to promote peace in the region and beyond. It is a selfless devotion to peace and stability not only in oneself but in other smaller and relatively weaker states. Because diplomacy works at its best when deployed positively to achieve peace, stability, and security. History is replete with examples of positive diplomacy that have proved to be a game-changer in maintaining and sustaining peace and stability.

Without going too far back, one can appreciate a relatively smaller state Qatar's role in facilitating the US and Afghan Taliban dialogue which led to a landmark Doha Agreement signed on February 29, 2020. At the time, Qatar itself was under a total blockade by the KSA-led quartet since June 5, 2017.

Yet Qatar provided the two parties with necessary wherewithal even though the US had never recognized Taliban as the Afghanistan's representative. Qatar proved itself as a responsible state among the comity of the nations and perhaps was rewarded also for being a peacemaker when the country faced an unjust blockade by the neighboring states.

Kuwait, a small Gulf country played a significant role as a peacemaker that averted a near-war-like situation in Qatar by a formidable regional alliance of Saudi Arabia, UAE, Bahrain, and Egypt, though an outsider. Kuwait knew the gravity of the situation on the morning of June 5, 2017, because it had been in a similar situation when Iraq's leader Saddam Hussain decided to invade a tiny neighbor on August 2, 1991.

Once again Qatar played a pivotal role in getting relief to Gaza City from the unjust and uncalled-for bombing of civilian targets including schools and hospitals. Qatar's role as a peacemaker in the region has been one of the causes of its blockade by its relatively bigger and stronger neighbors. However, Qatar's efforts for peace through positive diplomacy are recognized at different levels and therefore when the country faced an unjust blockade, its diplomatic efforts bore fruit and despite Saudi Arab and UAE's international stature, the international institutions did not support them.

Qatar again hit the headlines during the period of crisis, when the Emir of Qatar did not forget to send a message of condolences to the UAE Leader, on the sad demise of his mother.[6] The Emir ensured that diplomatic values were maintained even if the political environment was strained due to an unjust blockade of which the UAE was a leading accomplice. In fact, in the Arab culture, these gestures matter a lot.

The role of positive diplomacy in maintaining and sustaining peace and stability cannot be overemphasized. In this regard, another effort was seen in October 2023 when China brokered a breakthrough between Saudi Arabia and Iran.[7] China says that it will "continue to support countries in the Middle East in exploring a development path that suits their national conditions, strengthening communication and dialogue, adhering to unity and self-improvement, and realizing good neighborliness and friendship."[8]

It is necessary to mention that Saudi Arabia and Iran do not share friendly historical relations and have not had diplomatic ties since the killing of a Shi'ite Muslim cleric. "Saudi Arabia cut ties with Iran responding to the storming of its embassy in Tehran in an escalating row between the rival Middle Eastern powers over Riyadh's execution of Sheikh Nimr al-Nimr, an outspoken opponent of the ruling Al Saudi family."[9] China's role in bringing the two regional giants closer is part of its drive to foster cooperation and development across all regions.

In the South Asian context, Pakistan displayed positive diplomacy when it voluntarily released the captured pilot of the downed MiG-21 Bison of the Indian Air Force (IAF) on February 27, 2019. It may be recalled that the South Asian nuclear neighbors: India and Pakistan had a limited military engagement, initiated by IAF when it violated the Pakistani airspace on the night of 25–26 February 2019, and dropped bombs on locations allegedly used as terror training camps. Pakistan responded through PAF and shot down at least two combat aircraft whereas the third helicopter was downed by friendly fire. However, the voluntary return of the captured pilot Wing Commander Abhinandan was not responded to positively by India and its leadership continued to follow an aggressive path and illegally absorbed the state of J&K through Parliamentary Amendments in its Constitution by abrogating article 370 and 35A which gave a special status to the J&K.

The US played positive diplomacy in the South Asian context, particularly since the overt nuclearization of the region in 1998. On each occasion of heightened tension during the Kargil Conflict of 1999, the Twin Peak Crisis 2001–2002, the Mumbai Attacks 2008, and even in February 2019 limited military engagement between India and Pakistan, the US was instrumental in averting a direct military engagement between the nuclear neighbors.

Going back into history, one finds how Pakistan played "its role during that period and how President Yahya Khan, acted as a go-between China and the US, communicating secretly with Chinese Prime Minister Zhou Enlai and President Richard Nixon, which led to Dr. Kissinger's path-breaking journey in a PIA plane from Islamabad to Beijing on July 9, 1971."[10] The positive diplomacy done by Pakistan at the time perhaps changed the architecture of the international system.

Since diplomacy has many avenues to play its part: economic to cultural, military to ideological, therefore it must remain positive in its efforts when it comes to attaining, maintaining, and sustaining peace, stability, and security is concerned.

## Negative Diplomacy

Negative diplomacy can be extremely dangerous for peace and stability either in the regional context or in the global context. States may conspire against each other to further their interests which could be harmful to the other state.

Not too far back in history, the UAE displayed a shade of negative diplomacy even before the Qatar blockade became effective, and it was later revealed that on February 5, 2017, "Daniel Kawczynski, a British parliamentarian, was paid 15,000 British pounds ($20,700) to help organize an anti-Qatar conference in London ... At the time, analysts described the conference as an attempt to gather support for a coup in Qatar and accused Saudi Arabia and the UAE of funding it."[11] Such an act of negative diplomacy lead to an uncalled-for blockade of a relatively smaller neighboring state.

In the South Asian context, India played negative diplomacy against Pakistan when it influenced the members of the FATF to keep the country on the Grey List even after it had complied with necessary legislation. The same was accepted by India's External Minister as quoted by Indian news agency ANI. Jaishankar said: "Due to us, Pakistan is under the lens of FATF and it was kept in the grey list."[12]

Likewise, the US played negatively when it came to the voting of United Nations Security Council (UNSC) Resolutions for the ceasefire by Israel in Gaza. On each occasion the Resolution was put to vote, the US vetoed it thus giving Israel a waiver to keep bombing schools, hospitals, and public places without any significant protection. This implied that the US was an accomplice of Israel in committing genocide of the Palestinian people in Gaza and elsewhere. The Biden Administration played an extremely negative role which was not expected by a sole superpower that it would veto a ceasefire resolution of UNSC.

On other occasions too, the US engaged itself in negative diplomacy when it prompted Ukraine with military and financial support to continue its war against Russia, instead of any effort toward war avoidance or conflict management. One expected the sole superpower to play its due role in averting wars and conflicts to ensure peace, stability, and security in the conflict-ridden region. Likewise, in Asia-Pacific's tense geopolitical and geostrategic environment, Nancy Pelosi's visit to Taiwan was a part of negative diplomacy, because the US has officially accepted the One China policy. Due to this visit, "this month, tensions in the Taiwan Strait reached levels not seen in nearly 30 years. In response to U.S. House Speaker Nancy Pelosi's visit to Taipei, Beijing launched joint military exercises around the island and suspended or canceled eight official military dialogues and cooperation channels with the United States."[13]

Going back into history, one finds that the US played a negative role in the establishment of strategic stability in South Asia. When India conducted its first atomic test, codenamed 'Smiling Buddha' in 1974, Pakistan was slapped with economic and military sanctions alongside India. It happened at a time when Pakistan had been dismembered by India's intervention in its internal affairs which led to an all-out war and the creation of Bangladesh. The US sanctions proved fatal for the remaining part of Pakistan's national security because it could not get the new fighter jets from Sweden, an atomic reprocessing plant from France, and A7 Bombers from the US. The denial of this essential hardware led to increased instability at the strategic level in South Asia and forced Pakistan to acquire an atomic bomb covertly to ensure its territorial integrity and sovereignty. The situation was only reversed when the erstwhile Soviet Union invaded Afghanistan in December 1979, and the US needed Pakistan's support to defeat a superpower.

## Hybrid Mannerism of Diplomacy

Diplomacy has many facets and multiple avenues. It may begin with bilateral relations with neighboring states and end at concluding no war agreements between the two to ensure that peace, stability, and security are attained, maintained, and sustained. Conversely, the neighboring states have disputes of such nature that they remain at odds for decades without even considering conflict resolution as a probability and continue to manage the conflict through diplomacy and deterrence. Whenever the two fail to deliver, the conflict turns into a military engagement of a diverse nature, all-out, limited, or hybrid.

One example of such a strained relationship is that of India and Pakistan, the two nuclear neighbors in South Asia. The two states have a long history of wars and conflicts over the past seven decades where the agenda of conflicts has risen to alarming levels. It all started with a dispute over the accession of the State of J&K. As per the two-nation theory, the Muslim-majority state was supposed to join Pakistan, but its non-Muslim Ruler decided to accede to India against the wishes of the people. The two states have had multiple wars over J&K before becoming nuclear weapons states, and numerous near-war and limited military engagements after declaring themselves as non-NPT nuclear weapons states.

The two nuclear neighbors are just managing their affairs in a risky manner and without any consideration of adopting a conflict resolution approach. Both India and Pakistan are relying on hard-core nuclear deterrence to avoid an all-out conventional and nuclear war but making no use of multiple avenues of diplomacy.

The adoption of hybrid mannerism could avert a war and may have led them to confidence-building measures (CBMs) that were at one time paving the way for conflict resolution before they were interrupted and discontinued soon after the Mumbai Attacks of 2008.

These unique characteristics of hybrid mannerism allow diplomacy to deploy a wide range of options to achieve its objectives. If the bilateralism is not working, multilateral forums can be activated. In the case of Qatar, one can see that the small Peninsular state thwarted all attempts of much larger adversaries and sailed through the long period of crisis without compromising on its principled stance and without firing a single bullet just by the skillful deployment of all avenues of diplomacy. In South Asia, this part of diplomacy is missing, and reliance on deterrence alone has caused several hot and cold limited military engagements.

## International Forums for Common Good

Diplomacy strives to attain, maintain, and sustain peace, stability, and security at all levels, yet it remains a far-fetched idea under the realist paradigm. However, since the inception of the UN, efforts have been made to bring some sanctity to the international order. For this purpose, several international organizations and institutions are developed to provide relief to the relatively less developed, smaller, and weaker states. Some of the international avenues of diplomacy that are open to all member states are briefly explained in the following paragraphs.

### The Charter of the United Nations

The Charter of the United Nations was established to save "succeeding generations from the scourge of war." The most important elements of the Charter include the Secretariat, the General Assembly, the Security Council, the Economic and Social Council, the International Court of Justice, and the Trusteeship Council. The Charter called for the UN to maintain international peace and security, promote social progress, ensure better standards of life, strengthen international law, and promote the expansion of human rights.

## The Vienna Convention on Diplomatic Relations

This treaty, adopted in April 1961 and first implemented in April 1964, codifies rules that have been established in customary law over centuries for the exchange and treatment of envoys between states. The document addresses the conduct of foreign relations and stipulates that diplomats can conduct their duties without the threat of influence from host governments. Its rules were intended to facilitate friendly relationships between nations irrespective of their differing governmental and social systems. While the treaty requires diplomats to follow foreign laws, the only sanction permissible under the Convention, in the absence of a waiver of immunity, is expulsion. This safeguards diplomats against abuse by local authorities. Reciprocity also underpins sanctions for the observance of the treaty. However, the Convention remains confined to providing protocols only for diplomatic staff. As a result, as part of a hybrid threat tactic, powerful nations can manipulate diplomats from relatively smaller states.

## Universal Declaration of Human Rights

The Universal Declaration of Human Rights (UDHR) was adopted by the UN General Assembly in December 1948 in response to the mass casualties of WW II. The UDHR provided a global road map for freedom and equality for all individuals. The document was prepared by countries from a range of regions with differing ideologies, including the USA, Lebanon, China, Australia, Chile, France, the Soviet Union, and the UK. This allowed the UDHR to benefit from contributions across many states and their diverse religious, political, and cultural contexts. The UN adopted the UDHR by resolution 217 A (III), with eight nations abstaining but none dissenting. However, despite the optimism of this declaration and its intended outcomes, human rights abuses still widely occur across the globe, including in Kashmir, Palestine, and many African countries, which poses questions about the implementation of the Declaration. Unfortunately, perpetrators of hybrid warfare do not concede to these Declarations due to the absence of other legal frameworks, and proper investigations against them.

## The Geneva Convention relative to the Protection of Civilian Persons in Time of War (Fourth Geneva Convention)

The Fourth Geneva Convention (GCIV) concerned humanitarian protections for civilians in war zones. Part III, Articles 27–141 of the Convention govern the status and treatment of protected persons. These provisions distinguish between the situation of foreigners within a territory of one party to a conflict and that of civilians in occupied territories. However, violations of the Convention are regularly reported from disputed territories such as Kashmir and occupied Palestine. Thus, a collective feature of all four Geneva Conventions and their additional Protocols lies in the collective responsibility of all signatories, which is often not fulfilled by relatively stronger states. This stands in conflict with the fact that all parties have pledged "to respect and to ensure respect for the Convention in all circumstances."

This is one framework that, if implemented in letter and spirit, could significantly help in addressing hybrid warfare tactics imposed on relatively smaller states by a regional hegemon. Thus, efforts should be made to strengthen this agreement, and states should facilitate its implementation to work toward sustainable peace and the development of smaller states. For instance, the protection of non-combatants can be ensured under a hybrid warfare state implementing the Geneva Conventions and this may include men and women, children, and all those who are not involved in violence. Unfortunately, the perpetrators of hybrid warfare target such people to create unrest and alienate people against their government.

## The Convention on the Prevention and Punishment of the Crime of Genocide (Genocide Convention)

Adopted on December 9, 1948, this Convention codified the crime of genocide. This was the first human rights treaty adopted by the UN General Assembly with the sole purpose of codifying an international commitment to never again engage in atrocities such as those committed during WW II. Its adoption marked a crucial step in the development of international human rights and criminal law frameworks as they stand today. The definition of the crime of genocide, as set out by the Convention, has been widely adopted at both national and international levels, including in the 1998 Rome Statute of the International Criminal Court (ICC). Importantly, the Convention establishes the obligation of parties to actively prevent and punish the crime of genocide, including by enacting legislation and prosecuting perpetrators, "whether they are constitutionally responsible rulers, public officials or private individuals" (Article IV). This obligation, in addition to the prohibition on committing genocide, has been considered as one norm of international customary law and is thus binding on all States, whether they have ratified the Convention.

It is necessary to mention that International Conventions, if executed in their true spirit, are designed to protect people from the perpetrators of hybrid warfare, which does not have a well-defined framework for the purpose. Therefore, it is incumbent upon the stakeholders that such Conventions are respected and executed to protect innocent people from the persecution of the same people.

## Convention on the Reduction of Statelessness

This treaty, which was adopted on 30 August 1961 and entered into force on 13 December 1975, aimed to complement the 1954 Convention Relating to the Status of Stateless Persons. These two treaties were the foundation of the international legal framework to address statelessness, a phenomenon that continues to affect the lives of millions around the world. Although the Universal Declaration of Human Rights confirms that everyone has the right to a nationality, it does not set out any rules regarding specific nationalities to which a person is entitled. Henceforth, the Convention is the primary international instrument for the conferral and non-withdrawal of citizenship to prevent cases of statelessness.

The perpetrators of hybrid warfare at times may not create direct physical harm to the target population but create conditions that are not suitable for a dignified survival of the populace and hence it is forced to abandon its ancestor's place. These people could be internally displaced also and in certain cases, they are forced to give up their nationality and seek refuge in a foreign land. Thus, it is possible to address some of the dangers posed by hybrid threats with this treaty.

## International Covenant on Civil and Political Rights

The International Covenant on Civil and Political Rights (ICCPR) was adopted by the UN General Assembly in 1966 and came into force in 1976. The ICCPR is perhaps the key international human rights treaty for a range of protections for civil and political rights. The treaty stipulates that its signatories protect and preserve basic human rights, such as the right to life and human dignity; equality before the law; freedom of speech, assembly, and association; religious freedom and privacy; freedom from torture, ill-treatment, and arbitrary detention; gender equality; a fair trial; family life and family unity; and minority rights. The ICCPR compels governments to take administrative, judicial, and legislative measures to protect the rights established in the treaty and to provide effective remedies. Thus, the ICCPR, if deployed in its true spirit can protect relatively smaller states against larger and more powerful regional and extra-regional nations against hybrid threats. Because it relates to the civil and political rights of the people even if the state is subjected to hybrid warfare tactics. These fundamental rights are universal and protected under numerous other Conventions as well.

## International Covenant on Economic, Social, and Cultural Rights

Adopted on December 16, 1966, the Covenant on Economic, Social, and Cultural Rights (ICESC) came into force on January 3, 1976. Along with the UDHR, the ICESC is part of the International Bill of Human Rights and commits its parties to grant economic, social, and cultural rights to all global non-self-governing and trust territories and individuals, including labor rights, and the right to health, education, and an adequate standard of living. As of July 2020, the Covenant has 171 signatories. The ICESCR (and its Optional Protocol) is part of the International Bill of Human Rights, along with the UDHR and the ICCPR, including the latter's first and second Optional Protocols.

# Conclusion

The role of diplomacy in maintaining and sustaining peace, stability, and security cannot be overemphasized. Diplomacy can do what deterrence cannot do. Diplomacy can convince the adversary with positive assurances of mutual benefits and bring peace and stability even if military engagement is imminent. Some of the abovementioned international institutions are the outcome of intense diplomacy among the stakeholders and aim to facilitate the relatively smaller ones in attaining, maintaining, and sustaining peace, stability, and security in the region and beyond. While the bigger and stronger states do violate at times to draw benefits for themselves, international diplomacy serves as a platform to raise your voice and concerns.

Diplomacy played an important role in averting a war during the blockade of Qatar (2017–2020) by the KSA-led quartet and the same was clearly defined by the country's officials in interaction with foreign media during the crisis. Kuwait led the positive diplomacy campaign to avert another war in the region. Qatar's diplomacy in each domain: external relations and military, proved efficacious in its response to the unjust and uncalled-for actions of the brotherly neighbors.

Diplomacy helps develop a deep understanding of the state's interests and prevents ambiguities that may arise due to miscommunication or disinformation spread by the proponents of negativity. Diplomacy opens the gates for exploring endless opportunities to avert crises and resolve disputes. Diplomacy not only protects one's interests but also respects the same of others.

Diplomacy brings people together and creates space for cooperation in multiple domains. From public diplomacy to sports diplomacy, and religious diplomacy to cultural diplomacy, diplomats can do wonders to make things happen both positively and negatively. When deployed positively, diplomacy can help create probabilities of achieving peace, stability, and security even among the arch-rivals. However, if deployed negatively, diplomacy can lead to disasters, deaths, and destruction even between the allies, because there are no permanent friends and foes in international relations, but the interests only. This was eloquently stated by Lord Palmerston in his famous speech in the House of Commons. "We have no eternal allies, and we have no perpetual enemies. Our interests are eternal and perpetual, and those interests we must follow."[14]

Therefore, it is extremely important that states deploy positive diplomacy in a hybrid manner so that peace, stability, and security can be attained, maintained, and sustained across the globe. This may sound idealistic and a challenge to the realist paradigm, but it is certainly doable given the variety of new challenges that mankind is faced with including pandemics, climate change, food security, rising inflations, economic recession, growing population, and larger scale conflict-migrants.

## Notes

1 Arab states issue 13 demands to end Qatar-Gulf crisis, *Aljazeera*, July 13, 2017, https://www.aljazeera.com/news/2017/7/12/arab-states-issue-13-demands-to-end-qatar-gulf-crisis (accessed February 5, 2024).
2 Ibid.
3 https://www.quora.com/Did-Winston-Churchill-say-Diplomacy-is-the-art-of-telling-people-to-go-to-hell-in-such-a-way-that-they-ask-for-directions (accessed July 17, 2021).
4 *Diplomatic Dictionary*, U.S. Diplomacy Center, U.S. Department of State, https://americandiplomacy.web.unc.edu/2014/06/ten-principles-of-operational-diplomacy-a-proposed-framework/ (accessed on November 16, 2022).
5 Paul Kreutzer, "Ten Principles of Operational Diplomacy: A Proposed Framework," *American Diplomacy*, June 2014, https://americandiplomacy.web.unc.edu/2014/06/ten-principles-of-operational-diplomacy-a-proposed-framework/ (accessed on November 16, 2022).
6 Qatar emir sends condolences to UAE leader, *AFP*, January 29, 2018, https://www.thenews.com.pk/print/274483-qatar-emir-sends-condolences-to-uae-leader (accessed November 21, 2023).
7 China-brokered Saudi-Iran deal driving "wave of reconciliation," *Aljazeera*, August 21, 2023.
8 Chinese News Agency *Xinhua* reported on China's Foreign Minister Yi Wang's efforts for Reconciliation between KSA and Iran, on August 21, 2023.
9 Sam Wilkin and Angus McDowall, "Saudi Arabia Cuts Ties with Iran as Row over Cleric's Death Escalates," *Reuters*, January 4, 2016.
10 Kissinger recognizes Pakistan's role in establishing China-US ties, *Dawn*, March 22, 2021.
11 Anti-Qatar Conference, *Aljazeera*, https://www.aljazeera.com/news/2018/2/18/qatars-blockade-in-2017-day-by-day-developments (accessed November 20, 2023).
12 India admits it "ensured" Pakistan remains on the Gray List, *The Express Tribune*, July 18, 2021.
13 Paul Haenle and Nathaniel Sher, "How Pelosi's Taiwan Visit Has Set a New Status Quo for U.S.-China Tensions," August 17, 2022.
14 Lord Palmerston speech, House of Commons, March 1, 1848.

## · 5 ·
# AVENUES OF DETERRENCE

## Introduction

Deterrence, the concept and part of military strategy was hijacked by the nuclear strategists of the time since the advent of nuclear technology in 1945. Whereas the concept of punishment for crime and rewards for good deeds has been ordained in the Holy Books. The same has been referred to by Freedman in his book *Deterrence*. Therefore, neither the concept nor its application is new in the international system which is based on an anarchic system deeply rooted in power and security. Still, the concept remains at the center of academic debates and draws a wide-ranging interest among researchers. However, like security, deterrence also remains a contested subject and there is no one universal definition or execution technique that any state has adopted since time immemorial. States employ the concept of deterrence in a variety of ways after they have determined the deterrent value of oneself and the opponent. Relatively stronger nations rely on the material strengths of their military to deter the adversary whereas smaller states rely on the support of allies to achieve similar objectives.

During the Cold War era, the two security blocs: The North Atlantic Treaty Organization (NATO) and the Warsaw Pact countries were providing security cover to the members of the respective organizations. However, the members of two blocs led by the two superpowers did not engage directly in military conflict during the Cold War but the proxy wars continued unabated. It was the nuclear deterrence that helped in avoiding a direct military engagement between the US and the USSR primarily due to the establishment of Mutually Assured Destruction (MAD).

This chapter aims to highlight all the avenues of deterrence, as has been practiced historically by states, and are in practice now as well, in the following paragraphs.

## Conventional Deterrence

Since the establishment of MAD between the two superpowers of the Cold War era: the US and the USSR, NATO's reliance on conventional deterrence increased manifold for the defense of west Europe against the communist Soviet Union. Mearsheimer's work on conventional deterrence further explains this aspect. "A potential attacker's fear of the consequences of military action lies at the heart of deterrence. Specifically, deterrence—a function of the costs and risks associated with military action—is most likely to obtain when an attacker believes that his probability of success is low and that the attendant costs will be high."[1] His conclusions are noteworthy, "We may identify three theories of conventional deterrence. The first contends that deterrence is likely to fail when one side enjoys a significant numerical advantage in forces; the second focuses on the nature of the weaponry on each side, arguing that deterrence is least likely to be obtained when offensive weapons dominate; and the third views deterrence as a function of the specific strategy available to the potential attacker."[2]

However, to determine the efficacy of conventional deterrence, it is necessary to review the deterrent capability of each stakeholder. This author has lamented at least seven factors, C7 to evaluate the deterrent value of any state. However, the same tool is deployed on the avenues of deterrence differently to determine if conventional deterrence will avert a war between two non-nuclear states. The C7 has been explained briefly in (Chapter 2) to understand and evaluate the strengths and weaknesses of the state to determine the behavior of the state.

Historical animosity notwithstanding, warfare remains the most ancient form to resolve disputes, whereas the rest of everything has been transformed. Bilateral Treaties, Agreements, Multilateral Treaties, the League of Nations, and the United Nations have not been able to avoid or prevent wars between states with territorial disputes. However, the most painful military engagements are those that happen between UMPs, even if they are not for territorial disputes, particularly in modern times. The realists' worldview manifests wars and conflicts in all their forms in pursuance of power and security by respective states, primarily in their best 'national interests.' Historically, the most common reasons for wars between states have been for territory, independence, resources, support for allies, etc.

Most wars are fought for territorial claims, and control by occupation because "Possession is nine-tenths of Law."[3] However, when the Treaty of Westphalia was signed in 1648 to define the State and its boundaries, it was assumed that it would have settled the boundary issues between States. Perhaps, it held good only for the European states, because it led to regional powers' quest to occupy lands and territories in the regions, and beyond Europe. Hence, history revolves around two distinct phases of the State's expansion: the era of religious expansion to expand religious influence in maximum numbers of states, and in modern times, the era of colonial expansion to enhance political influence on extra-regional States.

## Nuclear Deterrence

Things changed after US President Truman decided to use its newest and deadliest weapon in history on the Japanese cities of Hiroshima and Nagasaki to bring WW II to an end in the Pacific. The Japanese cities were bombed with atomic weapons on August 6 and 9, 1945, respectively. The horror created by the atomic bombs changed the paradigm of security of states, and on the one hand, the race for the acquisition of similar weapons started, and on the other The Iron Curtain was dropped in the European theater. Two distinct blocs were formed: NATO and the Warsaw Pact, with differing ideologies, and thought processes on security. It was a matter of time that at least five states got the technology and claimed the status: the US, the USSR, the UK, France, and China. Consequently, Israel, India, Pakistan, and North Korea have become a de facto member of the nuclear club, and Iran remains an aspirant to join them.

The concept of deterrence changed, and academics and practitioners started to focus on enhancing the nuclear deterrent capability of respective states. States started to get nuclear coverage for security from the allies under the garb of extended deterrence and joined the distinct groups. The era of proxy war began with the establishment of MAD, and only one thing was ensured: the two superpowers, the US and USSR did not directly engage in a conventional war but always remained prepared with their Inter-Continental Bombers and Missiles.

Likewise, academics started to come up with theories on deterrence[4] and its efficacies for war avoidance due to the horrible consequences of its use. States started to wargame and instantly predicted an Armageddon, should the nuclear war take place. Perhaps, the fear of the known came close during the Cuban Missile Crisis (CMC)[5] in 1962 when the two superpowers came close to a nuclear war. CMC remains the most feared and widely discussed event of the Cold War era even after the passage of half a century. President Biden recently referred to CMC while critically analyzing the situation evolving out of the Russia-Ukraine war which has entered into the third year, with no end in sight. Rather, Russia's former President and Deputy Chairman of Russia's Security Council, which is headed by President Putin, has threatened to use nuclear weapons against Ukraine, "Just imagine that the offensive ... in tandem with NATO, succeeded and ended up with part of our land being taken away. Then we would have to use nuclear weapons by the stipulations of the Russian Presidential Decree," Medvedev further stated, "There simply wouldn't be any other solution, ... Our enemies should pray to our fighters that they do not allow the world to go up in nuclear flames."[6]

During the Cold War and that too in the post-CMC, the only second military engagement between two nuclear states, though limited in geographical space, was along the Ussuri River skirmishes between China and the Soviet Union (USSR) in 1969.[7] However, in the post-Cold War, The Kargil Conflict[8] led South Asia to be declared the most dangerous place in the world by US President Bill Clinton.[9] The nuclear equation in South Asia was meant to ensure that an all out conventional war was avoided, but limited wars due to protracted conflicts have continued at the peripheries causing concern about the potential horizontal or vertical escalation of conflict. The enduring rivalry between India and Pakistan has been changing—from all-out conventional wars in the pre-nuclear era to limited military engagements in Siachen, Kargil, and Balakot, under the nuclear overhang to an all-spectrum hybrid war spanning over two decades.

The traditional meaning of deterrence mainly focused on the cost-benefit analysis; capability, intent, and communication remained the most vital pillars of the concept of deterrence, and perhaps would remain so in the future also. The concept of deterrence served its efficacy by preventing the two superpowers: the US and the USSR from directly engaging themselves in an armed conflict during the entire Cold War era. However, the traditional meaning of deterrence seems to have lost its relevance in the India-Pakistan context where both the nuclear states continue to engage themselves in acts of subversion, propaganda, sabotage, alleged support for extremism and terrorism, preparation for limited war, military standoff, and sub-conventional warfare, etc.

Therefore, the possibility of conflict transforming into violent clashes remains highly probable as the asymmetry increases, because between the two nuclear nations, "it is no longer possible to impose unconditional surrender at an acceptable cost."[10] This author fears an unthinkable situation about which Kissinger had cautioned more than half the century ago, "War between nuclear powers has to be planned on the assumption that it likely to be a nuclear war."[11] No matter how low its probability is, its possibility exists, and hence the possibility of peace would remain elusive. Kissinger has categorically stated that "the degree of certainty, moreover, must be almost foolproof: a slight probability will not be sufficient, for the attacker is not just staking his chances of victory, but his national survival."[12] Therefore, the possibility of conflict transforming into violent clashes remains highly probable as the asymmetry increases between the two nuclear nations.

That means early definitions related to dissuading the adversary from not doing something desirable to a potential aggressor made stakeholders conscious of the possible consequences. Subsequently, as the concept matured coercion became more pronounced. However, the concept in its essence conveys in clear terms that the consequences of an undesired action would be such that the potential attacker would in the end gain nothing. The same was very well understood by the Cold War rivals, hence they avoided a direct military engagement during the entire period and instead used their proxies to fight their wars. However, South Asian leaders do not seem to consider the consequences and therefore do not hesitate to posture, threatening, and even physical military action, challenging the so-called nuclear deterrence.

## Extended Deterrence

While the concept of allies giving cover to each other against a common enemy is as old as the warfare itself, the concept of extended deterrence emerged as part of the Cold War package to provide a safety net to the US allies against the potential threats by the Soviet Union.

The concept emerged with nuclear deterrence gaining ground with the fears of nuclear proliferation. "The US employs extended deterrence daily to project deterrent effects in key regions across the globe. These forward-deployed assets combined with the global reach of continental United States (CONUS)-based nuclear forces provide theater-level assurance to allies abroad and deterrence to adversaries."[13]

The formal document of USAF doctrine states that during the Cold War, several US allies feared attacks from the erstwhile Soviet Union and hence had to be provided with a safety net commonly referred to as extended deterrence. Initially, the policy was based on the doctrine of massive retaliation, however, even after the establishment of MAD, it remains a cornerstone of the security net for the allies, particularly South Korea, Japan, and Australia.[14]

However, in the contemporary environment where the international system might be heading for a multilateralism. Therefore,

> "Today, a logical and sensible case can be made for extended deterrence which need not encompass threats of first use. Frontline countries such as Taiwan or South Korea may well wish to remain under the US umbrella, but it does not necessarily follow that they also wish the Pentagon to base its deterrent strategy . . . . Given the weight placed on the putative association between first use and extended deterrence by conservative analysts and the frequency with which it is repeated, it is remarkable how little contemporary evidence there is for the link."[15]

However, nuclear weapons remain essential to the US policy of extended deterrents. "This 'nuclear umbrella' is central to the basic U.S. defense goal of assurance ... It is part of the basic security considerations of countries such as Japan, South Korea, and Turkey. The United States can decide if the assurance of allies is a worthy continuing goal, but only our allies can decide whether they are sufficiently assured."[16] Hence the concept of extended deterrence remains valid for the time being and in the coming decades.

## Ideological Deterrence

Ideology plays an important role in shaping the policies of the state, particularly those which are purposefully built: Israel and Pakistan. These two states came into being to practice a particular religious ideology. Israel is a Jewish state, whereas Pakistan is an Islamic Republic. Hence, the two states give preference to religious ideologies while making state policies. That does not mean that other states do not have religious or nationalistic ideologies. For instance, during the WW II, Japanese Kamikaze. "The word *kamikaze* means "divine wind," a reference to a typhoon that fortuitously dispersed a Mongol invasion fleet threatening Japan from the west in 1281. Most kamikaze planes were ordinary fighters or light bombers, usually loaded with bombs and extra gasoline tanks before being flown deliberately to crash into their targets."[17]

Likewise, India's Prime Minister Indira Gandhi was assassinated by her guards who belonged to a religious community: Sikh, who was out to take revenge for her actions against an army raid on their sacred temple in Amritsar in June 1984. Indira Gandhi was killed on October 31, 1984, after which riots broke out, and thousands of innocent Sikhs were killed under the garb of Hindu revenge. This unfortunate history was repeated in India when Indira Gandhi's son and "former Indian Prime Minister Rajiv Gandhi was assassinated by the Liberation Tigers of Tamil Eelam (LTTE) on 21 May 1991. He was killed at a place called Sriperumbudur in the south Indian state of Tamil Nadu. Death came in the form of Dhanu a young Tamil woman from Sri Lanka,"[18] who carried out a suicide attack, instantly killing Gandhi and 14 others. This attack was also under ideological influence because he committed during his election campaign that if he returned to power, he would deploy Indian Peace Keeping Forces (IPKF) to disarm LTTE in Sri Lanka. These two assassinations of mother and son, both served as Prime Ministers of India, were undertaken under ideological influences: the mother was killed by members of the Sikh community, and the son was killed by the Tamil community of Sri Lanka, due to their perceived policies against a particular religious community.

Ideological influences can act as a credible deterrence against their adversaries. Israel's strength lies in its ideology and its values for which it can go to any length. The entire Arab world and Muslim states together with many other states keep criticizing Israel for Jewish settlements on the Palestinian land, but it ignores them and does what it wants, primarily because its military strength supports its ideological deterrence for the rest.

Likewise, Pakistan uses its ideology to motivate its armed forces to train, deploy, and become martyrs for the sake of the country, which is the Islamic Republic, and the fight is against the infidels. Ideology is a great asset with Pakistan's Armed Forces against the five-times larger India. The South Asia rivals have had numerous wars and conflicts in their enduring rivalry since the British left the Sub-continent in August 1947. India does care about Pakistan's ideological deterrence, perhaps more than nuclear deterrence, because the same has had numerous failures since the two declared themselves as de facto nuclear states in 1998.

## Economic Deterrence

Interestingly, this avenue of deterrence is least discussed in academia but remains the most effective tool that developed countries have through International Financial Institutions (IFIs). Toward the end of WW II, the Allies were crafting a new World Order to control global affairs, and they certainly needed a few international institutions that would have recognition of other countries. The Western world leaders met at Bretton Woods, New Hampshire from July 1 to 22, 1944. Some 44 countries attended the conference and agreed to "a series of new rules for the post-WWII international monetary system. The two major accomplishments of the conference were the creation of the International Monetary Fund (IMF) and the International Bank for Reconstruction and Development (IBRD)."[19] The two most important and effective pillars of the Conference meeting resulted in the founding of the IMF and the World Bank, twin intergovernmental pillars supporting the structure of the world's economic and financial order. The World Bank finances economic development, while the IMF oversees the international monetary system.

The IMF and the World Bank are effectively used as tools of economic deterrence through engagement against states that are either declared rouge or violating international norms and practices. Dong in his essay suggests three strategies of economic deterrence: punishment, denial, and diminution. He also "suggests that economic engagement can be employed to advance the ability, credibility, and communication for economic deterrence, as well as to create favorable conditions to adopt the three economic strategies."[20]

The global players, particularly the US uses economic sanctions very frequently and effectively against the states that are perceived to violate human rights, money laundering, terror financing, and are engaged in militaristic activism, including nuclear proliferation. Now also, the US has imposed a wide-ranging sanction on Russia for the Ukraine War, Iran for nuclear ambitions, and North Korea for nuclear proliferation.

Another important global institution that deters the states involved in illegal acts is "The Financial Action Task Force (FATF) leads global action to tackle money laundering, terrorist and proliferation financing. The 40-member body sets international standards to ensure national authorities can effectively go after illicit funds linked to drug trafficking, the illicit arms trade, cyber fraud, and other serious crimes."[21] Established with great purpose, FATF has been used against states for political strangulation, at times. Pakistan has been a victim of FATF since 2017, when it was placed on the Grey List and despite compliance, India lobbied and persuaded the institution to keep the country on the Grey List to cause harm, as part of its hybrid war. The same was accepted by an Indian External Minister S Jaishankar admitted, "Due to us, Pakistan is under the lens of FATF, and it was kept in the grey list."[22]

The unfortunate part of all these international institutions is that they act as the frontmen of the US-led leading players and are used as political tools of economic deterrence. For instance, Afghanistan's government under the Taliban remains unrecognized except China, even though the power was handed over to them after the Doha Agreement of February 29, 2020. The US continues to hold the country's assets worth billions of dollars to pressure the regime for women's empowerment. Afghanistan is a tribal society and has its customs and culture to manage the affairs of women. This author by no means subscribes to the Taliban's acts of brutal handling of its female population but suggests that the new government needs time and politico-economic support of the world instead of economic sanctions. The US must understand that it could not deter Afghans in its two-decade-long occupation then how can it do it alone through economic deterrence once it left the country in haste after an agreement?

## Colonial Deterrence

Interestingly, this terminology may not be found in academic writings per se but remains an effective deterrent tool with the colonial masters over their former subjects, particularly in Africa, even after the colonial Empires were theoretically abolished. This type of deterrence is effective in shaping the former colonies' policies, particularly those that relate to mineral extraction and economic development. Since there is a lot of corruption in those countries, it is easy to select and install the regime of choice and get the jobs done from those people.

Briefly, the major European powers of the time: Britain, France, Germany, Portugal, Spain, Belgium, and Italy, shared the number of African countries during the colonial era. These powers not only imposed a direct rule and occupied the territory and resources, but also imposed their language, culture, laws, regulations, and ways of living and doing business. Without going into the debate whether African countries would have developed faster without colonization, or they are better off today after being colonized, this author is of the view that why has the colonial era not ended in Africa, as has in other parts of the world. Why do former colonial masters still have regimes of their choice, and why do they punish the states that are trying to get real independence? Historically, the aim of colonialism was:

> To exploit the physical, human, and economic resources of an area to benefit the colonizing nation. European powers pursued this goal by encouraging the development of a commodity-based trading system, a cash crop agriculture system, and by building a trade network linking the total economic output of a region to the demands of the colonizing state. The development of colonialism and the partition of Africa by the European colonial powers arrested the natural development of the African economic system.[23]

This author opines that the colonial masters still controlled the situation in their erstwhile colonies. "Any careful analysis will show that British colonialism still plays a major role in the tragedies and disasters we see in Africa today. Take the migrants' deaths in the Mediterranean, and the continued hardline policies being pursued by the British government toward migrants, and say this is not colonialism at its worst … These are colonial era tactics, still employed with regards to who controls the revenues from Africa."[24] However, the Global South, now led by China may usher in a new era of real independence for the African nations before they are recolonized by another rising power, China.

## Cultural Deterrence

Perhaps, this is also new terminology or at least not commonly referred to in social sciences. Culture is one of the strongest factors in the approach and application of deterrence theories. It not only relates to strategic cultures but also to how deterrence is practiced or executed. The strategic culture of a society determines how that society or state looks at security matters and how it perceives the threat to prepare its response.

Theoretically, the developed democracies are considered rational in their approach, however, the US-led west has proved otherwise through its wars against the UMPs. Contrarily, authoritarian states have stayed away from wars and conflicts particularly in the 21$^{st}$ century except Russia's war on Ukraine.

It is interesting how cultural deterrence can add to the deterrent value of the state and avoid or engage in wars and conflict only due to this avenue of deterrence. For instance, Afghanistan's strategic culture is determined by the tribal nature of the society that does not accept foreign occupation under any conditions. In its long history of wars and conflicts that date back pre-colonial era, Afghanistan has successfully fought against and defeated at least three superpowers of the time: the British, the Soviets, and the Americans. This author opines that the series of these victories will now act as cultural deterrence for any future intruders onto Afghan soil. Afghan society loves weapons and wars. They do not initiate a war but do not accept defeat and the same has been proven multiple times in history. At least over the past 50 years, the country has been relentlessly bombed and destroyed by the two most powerful nations: the US and the USSR, but Afghan society valiantly resisted occupation and continued fighting until the invaders left the country. They may have engaged in civil wars for the supremacy of a particular ethnic group but that does not mean that they will not join hands against the foreign occupiers.

Another region that may be included in the category of creating deterrence based on the strong culture could be the ASEAN region. The region is comprised of ten independent and sovereign states that include Brunei Darussalam, Cambodia, Indonesia, Lao PDR, Malaysia, Myanmar, Philippines, Singapore, Thailand, and Vietnam. The ASEAN was established on August 8, 1967, but its Charter was officially enacted on December 15, 2008, with its Secretariat in Jakarta, Indonesia. It calls for mutual respect, non-interference, and commitment to the non-use of force to resolve any disputes among the member states.[25]

ASEAN is a peaceful region, and the population of the entire region is religiously, ethnically, and culturally diverse, with nearly no signs of discontent. The ASEAN has a few Buddhist nations, Muslim nations, and large Chinese and Hindu communities, but they live peacefully and participate in each other's socio-cultural functions enthusiastically. ASEAN is the best example of hybrid peace and productive engagement within and without.[26] Perhaps, Myanmar is the only state that creates waves due to gross violations of human rights, and the pursuance of ethnic cleansing of Rohingya Muslims. The ASEAN does not have a regional hegemon, though Indonesia is the most populace state and the largest Muslim country in the world. Brunei Darussalam is the smallest state and the richest, but none of the big players eyes on its wealth, as has been seen in other regions. Iraq's invasion of Kuwait may be referred to as a case in point.

ASEAN states thrive on the diverse nature of their makeup. Be it religious or cultural, nearly all states are considered tourist destinations. This author had the opportunity to lead an NDU study panel in Bali-Indonesia in 2012. The Governor of Bali was a Hindu because Bali is a Hindu-majority province in a Muslim-majority state, and he proudly briefed how peacefully he manages the issues related to places of worship in this tourists' heaven, famous for its beaches.[27]

This author opines that cultural diversity has added to deterrent value among the ASEAN nations and it would be extremely difficult to penetrate this united front if the situation so arrives in the future.

## Regional Deterrence

The terminology of regional deterrence may not be found in the literature, but it remains in practice across all regions. Several subregions have attained, maintained, and sustained peace, stability, and security through multiple bilateral and multilateral agreements. For instance, the ASEAN may not be a security alliance, but the region does have a peaceful outlook that serves as a deterrent to intra and extra-regional forces to avoid wars and conflicts. Regional unity in the face of ethno-cultural and religious diversity is an asset for the ASEAN region. Despite numerous territorial claims and conflicts in the South China Sea, the member states have resolved to adopt conflict management approaches that have ensured no mentionable trouble between any member states in decades.

Likewise, the South American states, though not equal in size, population, and natural resources, and have cultural diversity like that of ASEAN, do carry an essence of regional deterrence in theory and practice. However, this author opines that non-military pacts in such regions carry a different type of deterrence that has a hybrid flavor more so in the non-kinetic domain. In such cases, the intra-regional states do not engage themselves in military conflict and do not interfere in each other's internal affairs. This is a huge success of deterrence in the region because it calls for "peace within and peace without."[28] The nations that strive for peace within and peace without, have a deterrent value of its kind, and even if it fails due to aggression of the external forces, it is mitigated successfully by the allies in quick time. The Blockade of Qatar by the regional countries was a huge blow to regional deterrence but the besieged state was rewarded with the unflinching support of other regional and extra-regional allies.

## International Deterrence

This could perhaps be the most effective deterrence to the perpetrators and violators of international rules, regulations, norms, and good practices if it were executed in true letter and spirit. International deterrence could be based on several international institutions and organizations that are primarily established to protect relatively weaker states. However, the international system is anarchic and selfish practicing the realist's paradigm, therefore, at times it may appear that international deterrence is failing. For instance, several wars and conflicts that are taking place in different parts of the world are the result of such failures, particularly against the UMPs.

The 21st century is riddled with wars and conflicts between the UMPs thereby causing deaths, destruction, and devastation. The primary reason is the failure of the international deterrence. The international law that was enacted to protect the relatively smaller and weaker states appears to be failing in its stated objectives. The UN failed to stop Russia from invading Ukraine and cannot undo Russia's gains into the Ukrainian territory. Likewise, the UN does not have the necessary wherewithal to stop Israel from committing genocide against the poor Palestinians; it cannot even pass a ceasefire resolution due to the veto power held by the Permanent Five (P5) members of the UNSC. However, it became extremely effective against Afghanistan and Iraq when it permitted unlimited military action by the US-led Western countries in the post-9/11 scenario. This only reflects that the UN cannot stop the powerful states from doing what they want to do, but it can successfully deter the smaller and weaker states at the behest of the powerful states.

## Geopolitical Deterrence

The concept of geopolitical deterrence or terminology may not be frequently used in the strategic literature; however, geopolitics remains a viable deterrent for the perpetrators. International organizations and institutions do have a deterrent value in terms of legal implications against mischief and the collaboration of creating peace and security situations. However, how is it different from the abovementioned international deterrence, and why has this author given it a separate heading?

Historically, the states, other than the superpowers of the time, who challenged the efficacy of geopolitical deterrence, were reduced to their size in the due course of time. For instance, Iraq's uncalled-for invasion of Kuwait not only led to the destabilization of the entire region but also provided an opportunity for the extra-regional forces to remain in the region for much longer than required. However, this did not happen in isolation, and it was part of the geopolitics of the time. Because "the U.S.-led response would set important precedents for the use of military force over subsequent decades."[29]

The Taliban government in Afghanistan refused to comply with international resolutions in a post-9/11 environment thereby challenging the geopolitical deterrence and suffering a twenty-year occupation and psycho-social and physical hardship. However, some states do not feel deterred by international order and do not care for UNGA Resolutions or even the ICJ observations, because they have unflinching support of the superpowers of the time. Israel has a history of not complying with UN Resolutions primarily because they are not binding and at the UNSC, they are well supported by the US which blatantly vetoes even the ceasefire resolutions. The ongoing genocidal acts of Israel against the unarmed Palestinians are a case in point.

This author opines that until a just international order for which the UN was established is ensured, anarchy will continue to rage, and peace, stability, and security will remain elusive concepts.

## Conclusion

The avenues of deterrence discussed in this chapter conclude that these may be deployed independently or in combination to deter wars and conflicts to accomplish peace, stability, and security. However, it may not suffice in the presence of a protracted conflict and active disputes between the warring states or the blocs. However, this author opines that if the deterrence is working particularly the military conventional or nuclear, at least a military engagement can be averted even if a lasting peace is not achieved.

Deterrence, being one of the oldest military strategies, has been partially successful, particularly since the advent of nuclear weapons. The establishment of MAD made sure that the two superpowers of the Cold War did not engage militarily, and they fought their wars through the proxies. This was the most unfortunate part of the Cold War history because a lot of lives were lost in the warring nations. This proves that deterrence alone cannot avoid wars and conflicts, and cannot guarantee peace, stability, and security of the relatively smaller and weaker states.

Therefore, an effort must be made to deploy both deterrence and diplomacy in concert to attain, maintain, and sustain peace, stability, and security in the region. These two terms or the tools that states have are inseparable and essentially required to avert wars and achieve peace, stability, and security between the two states thereby contributing to the same in the region.

## Notes

1. John J. Mearsheimer, "Conventional Deterrence," in *Conventional Deterrence*, 23–66. Cornell University Press, 1983, http://www.jstor.org/stable/10.7591/j.ctt1rv61v2.5.
2. Ibid.
3. https://www.lawteacher.net/free-law-essays/land-law/possession-is-nine-tenths-of-law.php (accessed May 18, 2021).
4. A brief overview of various relevant deterrence theories is placed in Appendix "A."
5. The Cuban Missile Crisis occurred in October 1962 following the placement of MRBMs by the Soviets on Cuban soil, which was perceived by the US as an imminent threat to its security. The thirteen-day crisis ended when the Soviet Union agreed to withdraw the missiles.
6. https://edition.cnn.com/2023/07/31/europe/medvedev-russia-nuclear-weapons-intl-hnk/index.html (accessed August 1, 2023).
7. The Sino-Soviet border conflict was a seven-month-long military conflict between China and the USSR in 1969.
8. The Kargil Conflict of 1999 between India and Pakistan took place soon after the two arch-rivals had declared themselves nuclear states. The Kargil Conflict had the potential for horizontal as well as vertical escalation and called for an immediate intervention by the US.
9. Jonathan Marcus, *Analysis: The World's Most Dangerous Place? BBC News* (London), March 23, 2000), http://news.bbc.co.uk/2/hi/south_asia/687021.stm (accessed November 13, 2013).
10. Henry A. Kissinger, *Nuclear Weapons and Foreign Policy* (New York: Harper & Brothers, 1957), 96.
11. Ibid., 199.
12. Henry A. Kissinger, *Nuclear Weapons and Foreign Policy* (New York: Harper & Brothers, 1957), 97.
13. Lewis Dunn, Gregory Giles, Jeffrey Larsen, and Thomas Skypek, *Foreign Perspectives on U.S. Nuclear Policy and Posture: Insights, Issues and Implications* (Defense Threat Reduction Agency, 2006).
14. Nuclear Operations, Air Force Doctrine Document 2–12, U.S. Air Force, May 7, 2009.
15. Wrestling with Deterrence: Bush Administration Strategy After 9/11, J.W. Knopf, Contemporary Security Policy, 29:2, 229—265, 2008.
16. John S. Foster, Jr. and Keith B. Payne, "What Are Nuclear Weapons For?" *Forum on Physics and Society of The American Physical Society* 36, no. 4 (October 2007).
17. https://www.britannica.com/topic/kamikaze (accessed August 2, 2023).

18 D.B.S. Jeyaraj, *The Assassination of Rajiv Gandhi by the LTTE*, May 20, 2023, https://www.dailymirror.lk/opinion/The-Assassination-of-Rajiv-Gandhi-by-the-LTTE/172-259541 (accessed August 2, 2023).
19 The Bretton Woods Conference, 1944, U.S. Department of State, Achieves, https://2001-2009.state.gov/r/pa/ho/time/wwii/98681.htm#:~:text=The%20Bretton%20Woods%20Conference%2C%20officially,post%2DWWII%20international%20monetary%20system (accessed August 3, 2022).
20 Dong Jung Kim, "Economic Deterrence through Economic Engagement," *Foreign Policy Analysis* 15, no. 2 (April 2019): 176–186, https://doi.org/10.1093/fpa/ory001. Published: March 16, 2018.
21 The FATF, https://www.fatf-gafi.org/en/the-fatf.html (accessed August 3, 2023).
22 India admits it 'ensured' Pakistan remains on the Gray List, *The Express Tribune*, July 18, 2021, https://tribune.com.pk/story/2311285/india-admits-it-ensured-pakistan-remains-on-grey-list (accessed August 3, 2023).
23 Joshua Dwayne Settles, *The Impact of Colonialism on African Economic Development*. Chancellor's Honors Program Projects (Knoxville: University of Tennessee, 1996), https://trace.tennessee.edu/utk_chanhonoproj/182 (accessed February 19, 2024).
24 Osaki Peebe Harry, "Colonialism in Africa Is Still Alive and Well," *The Guardian*, August 1, 2017.
25 Association of Southeast Asian Nations, https://asean.org/about-us/ (accessed February 3, 2024).
26 Zia Ul Haque Shamsi, *South Asia Needs Hybrid Peace* (New York: Peter Lang, 2022), 52–53.
27 Ibid., 53.
28 This author quotes Muhammad Ali Jinnah, Father of the Pakistani Nation in his book, *South Asia Needs Hybrid Peace* (New York: Peter Lang, 2022).
29 "Persian Gul War: 1990–1991," *Britannica*, https://www.britannica.com/event/Persian-Gulf-War (accessed February 20, 2024).

# · 6 ·

# EFFICACY OF DETERRENT CAPABILITY AS A GUARANTOR OF PEACE, STABILITY, AND SECURITY

## Introduction

The Chinese sage Sun Tzu some 2,500 years ago warned the emperor that one must not spend his energies thinking whether his enemy would attack him or not, but rather invest your efforts in the preparation of such defensive mechanisms that the enemy does not even contemplate an offensive action for the fear of unfavorable consequences. Perhaps, Sun Tzu was referring to credible minimum deterrence, the policy that Pakistan adopted soon after declaring itself as a nuclear power after 1998 tests, in response to India's stream of tests. However, the concept gained prominence in crafting military strategies, particularly during the Cold War era after its destructive power was verified when the US dropped the atomic bombs on Hiroshima and Nagasaki on August 6 and 9, 1945, to force a surrender on Japan.

Deterrence remains one of the most practiced military strategies in all its avenues, and therefore, this author is not deploying nuclear deterrence alone in the discussion. While NKW has gained more popularity in military strategy in the changed paradigm, economic deterrence through engagement and sanctions has assumed a leading role in punishing the target state. However, this kind of deterrence strategy fails due to the target state's refusal to comply, either because of its own ideological, and economic strengths, or the strong support of the Alliance partners. For instance, Qatar could not be tamed by the Saudi-led quartet when they imposed a blockade of land, air, and sea routes, of the tiny Gulf state on June 5, 2017. Qatar endured the blockade due to its economic strengths, leadership's resolve, public support, and friendly countries' support, with Turkey leading.

Likewise, Houthi fighters of Yemen refused to be deterred by the strong military action of the Saudi-led alliance and fought for eight years through sub-conventional warfare strategies, finally, the attackers announced a ceasefire, after an unnecessary war that pushed Yemen to ever famine and human rights crises.

Afghans do not get deterred, no matter who is challenging them. In the last four decades, they have faced occupation by two superpowers: the Soviet Union (December 1979-February 1989), and the US (October 2001–August 2021). During the period, thousands of Afghans died, millions migrated to other countries, country's infrastructure was destroyed; but nothing worked against them, and today the same people are ruling Afghanistan who were blamed and ousted from power after the 9/11 events in the US.

## Deterrence: What Is It?

While the concept of deterrence has been explained in the previous chapters, it is necessary to reiterate that deterrence as a premier choice of strategy, perhaps needs to be studied again due to its productivity because there is consensus that nuclear weapons are not useable due to their immense destructive power. In case nuclear weapons are used against a nuclear weapon state that has an assured second-strike capability, both will be destroyed completely and there will be no winners. Moreover, the use of nuclear weapons against a non-nuclear state may be extremely difficult due to an evolving international environment where the smaller states do have some kind of extended deterrence coverage by the superpowers.

This traditional meaning and concept of deterrence served its purpose in letter and spirit between the Cold War rivals: The United States (US) and the erstwhile Soviet Union (USSR), because they understood its consequences and perhaps learned some lessons after the Cuban Missile Crisis of 1962. Thereafter, the two superpowers of the time never clashed with each other directly and continued to exercise their military power in wars, conflicts, and crises through the proxies.

Whereas, in South Asia's nuclear equation, it is necessary to distinguish between the deteree and the deterred state. Generally, the relatively smaller and weaker state acquires deterrent capability due to an existential threat. Pakistan's quest for nuclear capability was to deny another 1971 against India.[1] India was instrumental in the break-up of Pakistan in 1971 to create Bangladesh when the neighboring state successfully deployed nearly all elements of hybrid warfare to accomplish its politico-military objectives. India's Prime Minister proudly accepted in 2015 that he also played a part in the campaign.

India insists that there is space for a limited war under the nuclear overhang, primarily to push back Pakistan's development by 10–12 years through a short, swift, and destructive war, within the nuclear threshold.

Back to deterrence, in 2019, if Pakistan was a deterring state, India did not feel deterred, and Balakot happened, no matter how poorly it was executed. Whereas, in 1999, if India was the deterring state, Pakistan was not deterred, and Kargil happened. As far as the execution of Kargil is concerned, it achieved a perfect surprise. However, the international and regional environment was not supportive of that kind of military operation soon after the nuclear tests in May 1998, first by India and then by Pakistan. Hence, Kashmir was at once declared the most dangerous place on earth by US President Bill Clinton. Moreover, Pakistan was labeled as the aggressor for which Indian diplomacy carried out an extensive exterior maneuver, whereas Pakistan lacked application due to various reasons. Pakistan's failure to achieve its politico-military objectives, despite initial successes through surprise and deception, greatly helped India to move closer to the US.

India seized the opportunity, provided by Pakistan, to initiate a 2+2 Ministerial Dialogue that lasted over two decades and culminated in an understanding of *Global Partnership and Indo-Pacific Cooperation*. Moreover, India signed a couple of Agreements with the US that would strengthen strategic cooperation between the two states, under Basic Exchange and Cooperative Agreements (BECA). Under the Agreement, India becomes eligible for access to state-of-the-art intelligence and communication tools that would enable it to receive real-time pictures in any future conflict with Pakistan or China.

However, strangely though, India and Pakistan do not consider each other's nuclear capability as an existential threat to respective states. For the South Asian rivals, the concept and essence of nuclear deterrence as pronounced by Bernard Brodie and many other Cold War theorists appears to have lost its true meaning. Yet, Henry Kissinger's remarks that nuclear nations do not plan only for a conventional war cannot be ignored but an attitude of 'will not happen.' Perhaps the understanding of South Asian leaders about the concepts of nuclear deterrence is entirely different from that of Cold War leaders. Unfortunately, South Asian leaders treat nuclear weapons, nuclear posturing, and statements of threats as normal; perhaps due to a lack of awareness of the possible consequences of a nuclear war, no matter how limited it is.

In the olden days, deterrence was meant to convince potential enemies that their actions would be met with serious consequences to the initiator.

Kenneth Waltz, a proliferation optimist, opined that the possession of nuclear weapons would keep the warring states away from wars.[2] Waltz appeared convinced that these weapons would provide relatively smaller and weaker states much-needed security against the relatively stronger and bigger adversary.[3] Waltz's views assumed that the leadership of warring states would think rationally and not even think of using such weapons. However, this concept does not seem to impress the South Asian rivals.

This author agrees with Ward Wilson's assertions that deterrence, like any other military strategy, does not operate without certain limitations. The stakeholders must think rationally about the costs of potential gains before they even contemplate its use or otherwise. Because it does not cover all situations.[4]

Thresa Delpech opines that "Leadership Lies at the Very Core of Deterrence."[5] However, she agrees that it may not be sufficient to ensure deterrence, yet an important factor. She asserts that at the time of the Cuban Missile Crisis in 1962, the Soviet leader Nikita Khrushchev assumed that US President John F. Kennedy was not experienced enough to deal with the crisis, and he would be able to deploy the missiles in Cuba without triggering a consequential response. However, the Russian leader failed to assess the institutional strengths of the US Administration that gave stability and wherewithal to its leadership to deal with such a crisis effectively.[6]

Therefore, it is necessary to understand that deterrence is a complex subject and requires a clear and comprehensive appreciation of the concept. Though the concept of deterrence is not limited to nuclear deterrence and conventional deterrence, since the advent of nuclear weapons, the terminology is mostly related to nuclear deterrence.

## Nuclear Deterrence: Averting Wars to Dare Not

This author is of the view that deterrence should reflect a sense of 'dare not' phenomenon in its intent and accomplishment of the purpose because the capabilities are well known to the rivals. A state that has a unique capability matched or unmatched across borders or held by its adversary must ensure that the opponent does not consider, think, plan, organize, or execute anything that could trigger a response from another capable state. Because failure to understand the concept in essence leads to wars and conflicts as stated earlier. However, this new definition of deterrence is fundamentally different from Israel's approach which is commonly referred to as the 'Samson Option.' Israelis believe that the nuclear deterrent could work, only if preparations for a Samson option could help convince the attackers that aggression would not prove gainful. "The 'Samson Option' refers not just to a last-resort spasm of pure national vengeance, but to a purposeful set of specific operational threats."[7] Israelis think it would be better to die with the Philistines than to die alone. However, "when examined together with Israel's still intentionally ambiguous nuclear strategy (a doctrine most commonly referred to as Israel's "bomb in the basement"), it becomes evident that these carefully fashioned threat postures are designed to enhance Israeli nuclear deterrence."[8]

This author's definition of deterrence 'dare not' is intended to add value to the words and capabilities of a nuclear state against its adversary regardless of its intent and capabilities. The phenomenon of limited wars under the nuclear overhang within the nuclear threshold should be done away with for a greater cause of a certain peace and not an uncertain living with crisis management alone. Pakistan must project its capability in a manner that Indians are made to believe that any attempt aimed at destabilizing it as a politico-economic entity, would be responded with unacceptable blows.

While proposing this definition of deterrence with the phrase 'dare not' this author is mindful of the fact that it would need to be supported by a strong leadership with a resolute political will alongside a highly sophisticated command and control system to manage its nuclear inventory. Pakistan must not let its diverse nuclear capability go without any worthwhile impression on its arch-rival India which at will threatens to annex its territories as and when required. India must not be allowed to make use of its conventional strengths to impose its will on Pakistan to accept its prescription of dispute resolution. Pakistan seems to have understood India's ploy and hence pronounced its nuclear strategy under the blanket term 'full spectrum deterrence'[9] meaning that the state must be capable of deterring the adversary in all domains: strategic, operational, and tactical. However, the capability needs upgrades due to technological developments, and consequently, the strategy calls for a serious review due to a changed paradigm.

Unfortunately, India does not regard Pakistan's nuclear capability seriously and keeps threatening of dire consequences for its unfounded support in the sub-conventional domain, and therefore blames Pakistan for any acts of terror inside its held territories without any investigations or evidence. This situation is far more serious and challenging, and therefore the global powers must intervene to help India-Pakistan resolve its disputes instead of just managing them, without waiting for the next military engagement, no matter how limited it is. Therefore, this author thinks that Pakistan would soon adopt the nuclear status of "Ready Deterrence" under its strategy of full spectrum deterrence, instead of "Recessed Deterrence" or "Non-Weaponized Deterrence."[10]

Why is it necessary to redefine deterrence in the changed paradigm? A lot of time has passed since deterrence was defined under bipolarity in the Cold War era. Though the concept may remain like what has been pronounced by Brodie onwards, the operational definition needs a paradigm shift. While the regimes and governments can be deterred through economic strangulation or the threats of political instability, people do not feel deterred by any level of threat. Social media has given the common man enough awareness that he/she can express himself/herself about the policies of his/her state as well as other states.

Today, the Russia-Ukraine war is more than two-years-old with no end in sight. Is it not the failure of deterrence? Russia did not feel deterred by US-led NATO and invaded Ukraine at will. On the other hand, Ukraine does not feel deterred by the Russian might and continues to resist, though due to the strong support of NATO.

Elsewhere also, the traditional meaning of deterrence is losing its relevance. Afghanistan faced a two-decade-long war against the most advanced and powerful military machine without giving up and ultimately ousted the occupiers to earn a well-deserved independence once again. Likewise, Houthis did not feel deterred by the KSA-led military alliance and fought for eight years without giving up on their rights to defense. And, in the case of North Korea and Iran, neither the regime nor the people get deterred by military or economic tools. Likewise, the US failed to deter the respective leaderships in Iraq and Afghanistan and engaged in protracted wars draining its resources. Similar is the case with Iran and North Korea. Both these states did not feel deterred and continued their nuclear programs despite stringent sanctions by the US and other stakeholders.

Likewise, Qatar did not get deterred by the KSA-led quartet (UAE, Bahrain, and Egypt), and after over three years of break-up, the Arab nations have reunited again without any significant outcome. Each of the above situations will be analyzed in the subsequent chapters.

Deterrence denotes the situation where you are asking your adversary not to do what you do not want him to do, whereas compellence is a situation where you ask your adversary to do what you want him to do. According to Britannica,

> **Deterrence is** a military strategy under which one power uses the threat of reprisal effectively to preclude an attack from an adversary power. With the advent of nuclear weapons, the term deterrence largely has been applied to the basic strategy of the nuclear powers and the major alliance systems . . . . Thus, nuclear deterrence strategy relies on two basic conditions: the ability to retaliate after a surprise attack must be perceived as credible; and the will to retaliate must be perceived as a possibility, though not necessarily as a certainty.[11]

## Nuclear Deterrent Capability: A Guarantor of National Security?

States acquire nuclear capability for a multitude of reasons. One of the fundamental reasons is to enhance national security thereby ensuring their territorial integrity and sovereignty. However, in the changed paradigm, the deterrent capability does not rest only on one attribute. The same was proved once the Soviet Union lost its political identity and the member states declared themselves independent and sovereign ending its association with the erstwhile Soviet Union in 1991.

The concept of security has undergone a sea change in its essence, approach, and application. Traditional security is now entirely dependent on the elements and factors of non-traditional security, particularly human security. No matter how forceful the military establishments of the state are, the state remains vulnerable to external influences if the people's well-being is not considered a priority. This does not mean that the traditional security measures are to be neglected particularly if the threat perception so demands for any state.

Therefore, it is necessary to determine the attributes that account for the strengths and weaknesses of the deterrent value of any state. This author has developed a model to calculate the deterrent value of any state, nuclear or non-nuclear. This model is commonly referred to as C7+Political Will. C7 includes Capability, Capacity, Credibility, Communicability, Command, Control, and Conduct of any state.

The C7+Political Will is the combination of tangible and intangible elements of a country's hard and soft power that can determine the deterrent value of any particular state. This model or a tool to calculate the deterrent value can be deployed on either state: aggressor or the responder, alike. Moreover, it is important to calculate the deterrent value of both the aggressor and the defender or the responder from the viewpoint of the doability of a military operation which is a prerequisite to evaluate any war or conflict on the Possibility-Probability (P2) Model discussed in detail in Chapter 2. To understand and determine the efficacy of the C7 model, a comparative analysis of selected countries that are engaged in protracted conflict was undertaken and is tabulated below in Tables 1 and 2.

A brief explanation of each element of C7 about the South Asia rivals is appended below.

## Capability

India and Pakistan have a long history of wars and conflicts. Since the departure of the British in August 1947, both states have engaged in a protracted conflict over J&K, therefore, both states concentrated on the development of a strong military capability to meet the evolving situation.

The two countries spent enormous resources in building the capabilities of their armed forces even at the cost of human security. Now the two states have large standing armies, navies, air forces, and missile and nuclear forces. While Pakistan keeps itself prepared to face off against India, the latter aspires to challenge China, and it gets enormous support from the US-led Western world for the purpose.

## Capacity

India and Pakistan can deal with each other militarily as they have done for the past seven decades. The two states developed their nuclear and missile

Table 1: India versus Pakistan

| C7 | India | Pakistan |
|---|---|---|
| Capability | Nuclear Weapons State, Large Conventional Forces | Nuclear Weapons State, Relatively Smaller Conventional Forces |
| Capacity | India can absorb attacks and respond forcefully | Pakistan can absorb attacks and respond appropriately |
| Credibility | India keeps threatening Pakistan with dire consequences | Pakistan's responses are credible |
| Communicability | India has an exhaustive communication system | Pakistan has an elaborate communication system |
| Command | Command over the defense and foreign policy rests on Civilian leadership | Command over the defense and security policy rests in Military leadership |
| Control | Control over nuclear assets is exercised by the Civilian leadership | Control over nuclear assets is exercised by the Military leadership |
| Conduct | India's conduct has been questioned due to the nuclear material theft cases, human rights record, atrocities against minorities, and surgical strikes on Pakistan | Pakistan's conduct as a responsible nuclear state was questioned when it initiated the Kargil Conflict in 1999 |

forces to enhance their respective capacities. However, Pakistan may have capacity issues due to its poor state of economy, because India has grown its economy to the level where it can afford to have a limited war under the nuclear overhang.

## Credibility

The military establishments of South Asia arch-rivals are credible in the sense that none accepts any transgression into its territorial integrity. India proved that when Pakistan initiated the Kargil Conflict in 1999, and Pakistan responded to India's violation of its territorial integrity in February 2019. However, among the civilian leadership, some of the Indian politicians keep on issuing irresponsible statements regarding Pakistan's part of Kashmir, whereas Pakistani politicians usually avoid such rhetoric.

## Communicability

Both India and Pakistan have fairly advanced communication systems and make use of strategic communication to build a narrative. India does it better than Pakistan due to its media outreach, particularly in the present-day regime of the Hindu Nationalist government of Narendra Modi. Pakistan did well under the leadership of Imran Khan when he categorically stated that any misadventure by India would be responded to in the same way. Pakistan Air Force's response on February 27, 2019, to the violation of its airspace on February 26, 2019, by the Indian Air Force was aimed at re-establishing deterrence.

## Command

The command structure of the two nuclear neighbors stands on sound footing and has matured over the years. The two opposing armed forces are highly professional in their assigned missions. Perhaps, the difference lies in the civilian supremacy in the defense policy formulation in India, whereas the military establishment plays a more dominating role in Pakistan.

## Control

The control of the use of nuclear assets in theory and practice rests with the civilian government in India. However, in Pakistan, civilian leadership may have some say in theory, but the real control lies with the Pakistan Army. The development and deployment of nuclear and missile forces is carried out and controlled by the Pakistan Army which has jealously guarded this control over the past five decades and played a central in what Pakistan has today to deter its five-times bigger and larger armed forces of India.

## Conduct

Since the establishment of MAD between the Cold War rivals: the US and the USSR, it was an unwritten principle that the two nuclear-armed countries will not militarily engage directly. The theory of *Rational Actor Deterrence* worked well except for the events of the Cuban Missile Crisis of 1962 when the erstwhile Soviet Union placed its MRBMs in Cuba, thereby taking the risk of a nuclear war.

However, in South Asia, both India and Pakistan have acted irresponsibly at different times. India initiated the nuclear-armed race in South Asia when it carried out its first atomic test in the Rajasthan desert near Pakistan's international border in May 1974. Thereafter Pakistan's quest for a nuclear weapons program started and continued through covert means throughout the period of the 1980s. However, Pakistan did not carry out any tests until India resumed its tests in May 1998. Left with no choice, Pakistan responded and carried out its nuclear tests within days in the same month of May 1998.

Pakistan acted irresponsibly when it initiated the Kargil Conflict of 1999, soon after the nuclear tests. India responded with full force and Pakistan had to retreat primarily due to the US pressure. On the other hand, India's conduct has been questioned due to the nuclear material theft cases, human rights record, atrocities against minorities, and surgical strikes on Pakistan. IAF violated Pakistan's airspace on the night of February 25–26, 2019, to which PAF responded on February 27, 2019. PAF shot down two IAF fighter jets, whereas one IAF combat helicopter was shot down by friendly fire.

Now, the Korean Peninsula, the purpose of evaluating the deterrent value of the arch-rivals of the Korean Peninsula is to pitch the two states with differing status: one with declared nuclear weapons on its inventory and the other with an extended deterrence guarantee by the US.

A brief explanation of Table 2 is appended below.

## Capability

The military capability of South Korea is largely dependent on the support of the US, whereas North Korea has a large standing army of 950,000 men with another three million in Reserves. However, when it comes to the quality of equipment and training, South Korea's armed forces are far more sophisticated and professional due to the all-out support of the US. A US Official with vast working experience puts South Korea's military capability at a much higher state than North Korean capabilities in the military domain.[12]

South Korea's strong economy gives it an edge to enhance its capability manifold because North Korea's economy can ill afford the modernization plans of its large army which continues to operate Cold War-era Soviet equipment. However, North Korea's independent nuclear and missile forces add

Table 2: South Korea versus North Korea

| C7 | South Korea | North Korea |
|---|---|---|
| Capability | Non-Nuclear Weapons State with Extended Nuclear Deterrence by the US | Nuclear Weapons State, Relatively large Conventional Forces |
| Capacity | South Korea can absorb a conventional attack and respond forcefully but in the conventional domain only | North Korea can absorb a conventional attack and respond appropriately but does not have No First Use Policy of nuclear weapons |
| Credibility | South Korea does not have offensive designs, but the presence of US Forces does create a security-insecurity dilemma in the Peninsula | North Korea keeps on threatening and regularly issues threat warnings that lack credibility |
| Communicability | South Korea has the necessary wherewithal and a state-of-the-art communication system | North Korea also has an elaborate communication system |
| Command | Command over the defense and foreign policy rests on Civilian leadership | Command over the defense and foreign policy rests in the Kim Family dynasty backed by strong military |
| Control | Control over armed forces is exercised by the Civilian leadership | Control over the armed forces and nuclear assets is exercised by the Kim Family dynasty backed by a strong military |
| Conduct | South Korea is considered a responsible democratic state | North Korea is considered an irresponsible and authoritarian state |

value to its deterrent capability, whereas South Korea remains dependent on US support.

## Capacity

In the domain of conventional warfighting, South Korea has the quality whereas North Korea has the quantity. Perhaps both the rivals can fight a limited conventional war, but an all-out war would certainly see the unconventional weapons by North Korea which South Korea will not be able to handle without the unwavering support of the US. The US official accepts that "... the [North's] unconventional threat -- the nukes, the missiles, cyber capabilities, special operations forces -- are growing." South Korea has been able to modernize its armed forces due to its robust economy and can ward off a conventional threat from North Korea. However, no sooner the US enters the conflict to support South Korea, China, and Russia will certainly move swiftly in support of North Korea so that it does not have to employ its nuclear weapons fearing an existential threat.

## Credibility

South Korea is an established democracy, and its decision-making mechanism is fairly transparent and credible. However, North Korea is ruled by a family in an authoritarian manner where the decision-making is done by one man alone—Kim Jong Un. Therefore, the credibility of one man's decision as against that of a democratic institution will always remain under suspicion. There is always a higher probability of erratic and irrational decision-making by an authoritarian ruler than the collective wisdom of people's representatives. History is replete with such examples where one man's decisions led to wars and conflicts. Khrushchev's decision to position MRBMs in Cuba caused the Cuban Missile Crisis in 1962, Saddam Hussain's invasion of Iraq in 1992 led to Gulf War I, and more recently Putin's decision to invade Ukraine, are only a few examples that led to wars and conflicts.

## Communicability

South Korea has state-of-the-art communication system that they have developed indigenously as well acquired from the US. South Korea is a producer and exporter of advanced communication technology. Therefore, there is a high probability that they will not fall short of North Korea in this domain. The North Korean system is tight-lipped and mostly opaque, thereby increasing the probabilities of communication breakdown and miscalculations. Since the power matrix in the Korean peninsula is unique where one is a nuclear-armed state and the other has an extended deterrence by the sole superpower, therefore the communication mechanism mustn't fail between the two rivals.

## Command

The command structure of South Korean armed forces is well organized and remains on the pattern of the US. The decision-making mechanism is also transparent and is backed by the allies. North Korea's command mechanism is entirely different and remains under one man only. Interestingly, there have been hardly any reports of discord or discontent in the hierarchical command structure.

## Control

Similarly, the control of the armed forces rests with civilian leadership in South Korea, but the same is closely controlled by one man in North Korea. The development, deployment, and employment decisions of nuclear as well as missile forces remain with the Communist leader Kim Jong Un only. He has consolidated control over its conventional as well as strategic armed forces.

## Conduct

South Korea is a true democracy and conducts itself as a responsible state. However, North Korea is an authoritarian state and therefore, its behavior is that of an irresponsible state when it comes to security affairs. It conducts missile tests at will and without due consideration for other regional states' safety and security. It unilaterally withdrew from the Nuclear Non-Proliferation Treaty (NPT) on April 10, 2003, becoming the first country to withdraw from the treaty. Much earlier on June 13, 1994, North Korea had withdrawn from membership of the International Atomic Energy Agency (IAEA) as well.

## Conclusion

This chapter dealt with the efficacy of deterrent value as a guarantor of peace, stability, and security for any state. For this purpose, it was necessary to evaluate the state's deterrent value for which an academic model C7+Political Will was developed and deployed in this research. Two conflict-ridden regions with different statuses and statures of stakeholders were evaluated on the C7 model. One is in South Asia where both India and Pakistan are nuclear states and have a long history of wars and conflicts on the disputed territory of J&K.

The other is in the Korean Peninsula where North Korea is nuclear-armed but economically poor, but South Korea is economically rich with an extended nuclear deterrence by the US.

The C7 evaluation in each case needed to be complemented with a strong political will because, without unflinching political support, the military establishments alone may not be able to withstand international pressure on matters related to nuclear weapons. However, the situation in each of the discussed regions is interesting and unique in the sense that in North Korea's dictatorial style of governance, the civilian institutions do not matter. Likewise, in Pakistan's democratic setup too, the civilian leadership supports the armed forces unconditionally when it comes to matters related to security, perhaps due to capacity issues of the civil institutions.

Therefore, one can conclude that nuclear weapons do play a role in enhancing a country's deterrent value, but it alone cannot guarantee unchallenged peace, stability, and security for any state, particularly with protracted conflicts and active disputes. This author agrees with Scott D. Sagan, who rightly pointed out the gravity of the situation in South Asia due to nuclear weapons proliferation. He thinks that deterrence may fail and that is what we have seen in the last two decades.

While diplomacy aims to protect and promote the national interests of a sovereign state, deterrence ensures the territorial integrity and sovereignty of that state. The tools diplomacy deploys mostly fall in the purview of soft power, whereas deterrence has to show its muscles to convince the adversary that its undesirable actions would be counterproductive. Both diplomacy and deterrence may use threats and incentives at times, independently or concurrently, to achieve their objectives. However, the efficacy of the two, diplomacy and deterrence, is highly dependent on the skillful employment of diplomacy and the effective deployment of the deterrent value each state may have depending on its capacity to project its power. Since the two tools, diplomacy and deterrence, have nearly similar objectives, therefore, they must be employed in a hybrid manner either concurrently or sequentially. There is little doubt that given the objectives in the respective domains, diplomacy and deterrence, will have to complement each other to ensure that the other one delivers. For instance, an imminent war can be averted through proactive and intense diplomacy even if the deterrence has failed, however, the probability of a military engagement will increase manifolds if both diplomacy and fail to deliver. Therefore, it is necessary that at least one must deliver to avoid wars and conflicts, however, to attain, maintain, and sustain peace, stability, and security, both diplomacy and deterrence will have to deliver. This author opines that the hybrid employment of diplomacy and deterrence may be the most suitable manner to achieve the desired results.

## Notes

1. Pakistan and India had an all-out war in 1971 after which Pakistan lost its Eastern Wing, and Bangladesh was created by India.
2. Kenneth Waltz, *Spread of Nuclear Weapons: More May Better*, Adelphi Papers, no. 171 (London: International Institute for Strategic Studies, 1981).
3. Kenneth N. Waltz, "Nuclear Myths and Political Realities," *American Political Science Review* 84, no. 3 (September 1990).
4. Ward Wilson, "The Myth of Nuclear Deterrence," *Non-proliferation Review* 15, no. 3 (November 2008).
5. Therese Delpech, *Nuclear Deterrence in 21$^{st}$ Century: Lessons from the Cold War for a New Era of Strategic Piracy* (RAND, 2012).
6. Ibid.
7. Louis René Beres, "Israel and the Samson Option in an Interconnected World," *Modern War Institute*, November 16, 2018, https://mwi.westpoint.edu/israel-samson-option-interconnected-world/ (accessed August 5, 2023).
8. Ibid.
9. Debalina Ghoshal, Pakistan's quest for a full spectrum nuclear deterrence: Testing of the Babur, Défense info, March 28, 2021, https://defense.info/global-dynamics/2021/03/pakistans-quest-for-a-full-spectrum-nuclear-deterrence-testing-of-the-babur/#:~:text=Pakistan's%20nuclear%20strategy%20is%20premised,a%20conventional%20war%20with%20India (accessed on August 3, 2023).
10. Zia Ul Haque Shamsi, Nuclear Deterrence and Conflict Management Between India and Pakistan, (New York: Peter Lang, 2022), 9.
11. https://www.britannica.com/topic/deterrence-political-and-military-strategy (accessed July 310, 2023).
12. Jim Garamone, "U.S. Official Salutes South Korea's 'Very Strong' Military," *DoD News*, Defense Media Activity, https://www.jcs.mil/Media/News/News-Display/Article/1357402/us-official-salutes-south-koreas-very-strong-military/#:~:text=North%20Korean%20Military%20Capabilities&text=Just%20comparing%20capabilities%2C%20the%20official,the%20North%2C%E2%80%9D%20he%20said (accessed February 2, 2024).

# · 7 ·

# INSEPARABLE LINKAGE BETWEEN DIPLOMACY AND DETERRENCE

While deterrence might be losing its color, diplomacy continues to strive for peace and stability, within and without. However, to attain, maintain, and sustain peace, stability, and security, both deterrence and diplomacy will have to work in sync. Because the failure of the one may lead to conflict turning into an otherwise avoidable war.

Conceptually, in the criminology domain, the "deterrence theory works on three key elements: certainty, celerity, and severity."[1] The concept remains dominant in Western authors' definitions of deterrence. However, much like the criminal proceedings on the committed crimes, the states also have developed filters against the traditional deterring nations: the US after unilateralism, colonial powers, and the regional hegemons.

This author concludes that nuclear deterrence alone cannot impress the adversary whether the latter is a nuclear power or not. Iran, still not a nuclear power, has endured multiple sanctions by the US since the Islamic Revolution of 1979. One can argue that Iran is rich in hydrocarbons, but the kind of hardship the people of Iran have gone through is unprecedented. North Korea developed its nuclear capability under sanctions and amid fears of attacks by the US. Likewise, Pakistan continued to develop its nuclear weapons program under strict US sanctions and resisted all kinds of pressures when the country decided to carry out tests in response to India's tests in 1998. It may be necessary to mention that all these three states have strong ideological inclinations: Pakistan and Iran have the overwhelming majority of Muslims, and North Korea is a staunch practitioner of communist ideology.

Pakistan's military leader General Zia ul Haq, who ruled the country for a decade during the Soviet invasion of Afghanistan and is credited to have played an important role in the weakening of the USSR, which ultimately led to its dissolution, visited India to watch a cricket match between the two nations, as part of 'Cricket Diplomacy.' However, he used the occasion to employ ideological deterrence by threatening a five-times larger adversary of wiping out its religious identity: Hinduism. Zia's son Ijaz ul Haq, a parliamentarian himself, quotes Behra Manan, an Adviser to Gandhi, who states that while bidding on departure Zia said,

> Mr. Rajiv you want to invade Pakistan? Ok fine go ahead! But please remember one thing after that people will forget Changez Khan and Hilaku Khan and will remember Zia and Rajiv Gandhi only. Because it will not be a Conventional War. Pakistan may suffer annihilation but Muslims will still survive because there are several Muslim countries in the world. But remember there is only one India and I shall wipe out Hinduism and Hindu religion from the face of the earth! And if you don't order complete de-escalation and demobilization before my return to Pakistan, the first word of mouth I will utter will be "Fire"![2]

This was the first direct threat of the use of nukes in the sub-continent, Pakistan had still not tested its systems, whereas India had carried out its first atomic test in 1974. This was a classic use of a potential deterrent capability of a state that was facing a much larger opponent on its borders. Pakistan's military leadership skillfully deployed sports diplomacy in sync with a nascent deterrence. Soon after Zia's threat, India started to pull back its troops, and a near-war situation was averted. This was a combination of sports diplomacy and ideological deterrence because its military capability was yet to be tested.

Likewise, there is an inseparable linkage between security and deterrence. Because non-military aspects have an overriding factor in the national security of any state under the changed paradigm, and military security is just one element of deterrent capability that a state must acquire. In either case, deterrent capability acquired to ensure own security against a relatively bigger and stronger state, or expand influence onto relatively smaller and weaker states, will significantly play a role in the process. Therefore, it is incumbent upon academics, researchers of international affairs and strategic studies to logically, rationally, and dispassionately evaluate the state's deterrent capability to predict a future event, and perhaps help the decision-makers in strategic decision-making.

## Application of the P2 Model (Initiators/Attackers)

To determine the veracity of the title of this chapter "Inseparable Linkage between Diplomacy and Deterrence" it is necessary to test some of the selected wars and conflicts of the 21st century on the P2 model. It is reemphasized that P2 is a tool that can be effectively used for decision-making and scenario planning. Therefore, efforts will be made to determine whether a particular war or conflict should have been initiated by the attackers or not. Consequently, D2 will be deployed to determine the effectiveness of diplomacy and deterrence to see if the defenders or the responders did enough to ward off the threat of kinetic application by the perpetrators.

Table 3 shows the Russia's offensive on Ukraine on February 24, 2022. Table 4 shows Ukraine's response to Russia's offensive. Table 5 shows the Hamas attacks on Israel on October 7, 2023, and Table 6 shows Israel's response to Hamas' offensive.

Brief explanations of Table 3 are appended below. On the scale of possibility, it is necessary to look at the interests and the behavior of the initiating state. Ukraine was a red line for Russia as far as NATO's eastward expansion was concerned. Therefore, it was no surprise that Russia would invade Ukraine to annex the eastern regions which are populated by ethnic Russians, and hence not resist their inclusion into the Russian Federation as autonomous regions. Therefore, from the Russian perspective, it was highly desirable to invade Ukraine before it announced joining NATO because Russia considered NATO's presence on its borders as an existential threat to its territorial integrity.

Likewise, on the scale of preferability, from the Russian perspective, the attack on Ukraine was highly preferable at the time before Ukraine had joined NATO and its troops were stationed along the Russian borders. President Putin knew that his actions would not receive global favorability, but he did not care and went ahead with his plans to attack Ukraine and annex the ethnic Russian regions of Donetsk, Kherson, Luhansk, and Zaporizhzhia oblasts. However, he got full support from China's President Xi Jinping, which may have come as a surprise to the US-led Western world.

Table 3: Russia's Offensive on Ukraine on P2 (Possibility-Probability) Model

|  | Desirability | Preferability | Favorability | Political Will |
|---|---|---|---|---|
| Possibility | Highly Desirable from Russia's perspective. | From the Russian perspective, the attack on Ukraine was highly preferable to deny NATO on its immediate borders. | Russia's attack on Ukraine was highly unfavorable for the world in general and the US-led Western world in particular. | Russia's attack on Ukraine was an outcome of the strong political will of its leadership. |
|  | Doability | Capacity | Sustainability | Exit Strategy |
| Probability | If the tangible military elements are considered, an attack on Ukraine was doable by Russia. | Russia's military could attack and absorb the Ukrainian response even if it is supported by NATO. | Russia's war on Ukraine has entered into third year and Russia has proved already that it could sustain the military operations against Ukraine forces which have the outright support of NATO. | Russia's exit strategy remains ambiguous, and the end of war is not in sight. |

Russia's attack on Ukraine was an outcome of a strong political will to ensure that Ukraine did not join NATO, and President Putin had declared Ukraine as his red line. Hence, on September 30, 2022, Russia unilaterally declared its annexation of areas in and around four Ukrainian oblasts—Donetsk, Kherson, Luhansk, and Zaporizhzhia.

However, to determine the probabilities of Russia's actions, it was necessary to evaluate the tangible elements of a country's strengths and weaknesses. Russia's military capability particularly against a relatively weaker opponent like Ukraine suggests that an invasion was doable. The same has been proved with the Russian force's advance into the Ukrainian heartland. Despite exhaustive support by NATO in terms of training, equipment, and finances, Russian forces could not be contained and were able to annex the regions of their choice.

Likewise, on the scale of capacity, the Russian forces could attack and absorb the Ukrainian response even if it is supported by NATO. The war has already entered third year, and Russians are not showing any signs of stress either on men, material, or the politico-military will. Russia has proved that it could sustain the military operations against Ukraine forces which have the outright support of NATO. Moreover, the Russian leadership has been able to convince its military and people that their war on Ukraine is extremely necessary to ward off NATO from their immediate borders.

Lastly, regarding the exit strategy, the war has entered third year now and there is no end in sight. Due to the ongoing Israeli genocide of the Palestinians following the Hamas attack of October 7, 2023, NATO's overt support to Ukraine has reduced or gone in the background, however, on the part of the Russians, there is no respite for the Ukrainians. Russia's exit strategy remains ambiguous and perhaps it is exploiting the Middle East situation to its advantage to gain as much ground as possible. There is a high probability that the areas captured by the Russian forces will not be returned to Ukraine any time soon.

Having analyzed the possibilities and the probabilities of the Russian offensive against Ukraine on the scale of tangible and intangible elements, it is necessary to evaluate the Ukrainian response on the scale of diplomacy and deterrence (D2) model.

On account of diplomacy, Ukraine's leadership failed to visualize Russia's intent of a kinetic application and continued its efforts for the membership of NATO. Ukraine has a long history of relationship with Russia and should have understood Russia's red line, particularly after it annexed Crimea in 2014. Moreover, the Ukrainian leadership failed to understand that the US-led Western world was dragging them into a war against Russia, perhaps to make it Afghanistan of the erstwhile Soviet Union. Ukraine also did not visualize that NATO's help would not be enough to hold its ground against the Russian offensive, especially in areas that have much of the Russian ethnic population.

On the other hand, Ukraine could not deter Russia from launching the ground invasion primarily due to much smaller and relatively weaker armed forces. Perhaps, Ukraine assumed that NATO's support would act as a deterrent to Russia, and it would not invade the country, however, President Putin did not bother because he had declared Ukraine as its red line.

On the avenues of diplomacy, NATO engaged in negative diplomacy and kept on instigating Ukraine to stand firm against Russia instead of making

Table 4: Ukraine's Response to D2 (Diplomacy-Deterrence) Model

|  | Diplomacy | Deterrence |
|---|---|---|
| Ukraine | Ukraine's leadership failed to visualize Russia's intent of a kinetic application and continued its efforts for the membership of NATO. | Ukraine assumed that NATO's support would act as a deterrent to Russia, and it would not invade Ukraine, however, President Putin did not bother because he had declared Ukraine as its red line. |
| NATO | NATO engaged in negative diplomacy and kept on instigating Russia for the war instead of making any worthwhile diplomatic effort to avert an impending war. | NATO failed to deter Russia with all its might and President Putin rejected NATO's overt support to Ukraine. |
| The UN | The UN and all other international institutions failed to impress Russia due to a half-hearted diplomatic effort. Russia vetoed all UNSC Resolutions and did not care for General Assembly Resolutions. | Russia also did not feel deterred by the UN Resolutions and went ahead with its pre-planned invasion. In its third year of war, Russia has already annexed at least four Eastern regions of Ukraine which are populated by the ethnic Russians. |
| China | China remains committed to Russia's support because it feels that NATO must not be allowed to border with Russia directly, and there should be enough buffer zones to avoid a broader conflict in the region. | China did not feel deterred by NATO or the UN and remains committed to the Russian cause of keeping NATO troops away from direct contact with the Russians. |

any worthwhile diplomatic effort to avert an impending war. Perhaps, a war between Russia and Ukraine was in the US interest, although its European partners had to face the consequences in terms of the energy shortfall. The UN and all other international institutions failed to impress Russia due to a half-hearted diplomatic effort. Russia vetoed all UNSC Resolutions and did not care for non-binding General Assembly Resolutions.

In the domain of deterrence, NATO failed to deter Russia with all its might and President Putin did not care for NATO's warnings of a bigger conflict and an overt support to Ukraine. Russia also did not feel deterred by the UN Resolutions and went ahead with its pre-planned invasion. In its third year of the war, Russia has already annexed at least four Eastern regions of Ukraine which are populated by ethnic Russians including Donetsk, Kherson, Luhansk, and Zaporizhzhia.

China being an emerging global player was keenly monitoring the evolving situation and, in the end, it remains committed to Russia's support because it feels that NATO must not be allowed to border with Russia directly, and there should be enough buffer zones to avoid a broader conflict in the region. China did not feel deterred by NATO or the UN and remains committed to the Russian cause of keeping NATO troops away from direct contact with the Russians. It is necessary to mention that since the formation of the SCO on June 15, 2001, the two regional giants have developed much closer ties in the political and economic domain.[3] The "main goal of SCO was to strengthen mutual trust, friendship, and good-neighborliness between the member states, therefore, there was very little probability that China would oppose any action of Russia taken in its supreme national interest."[4]

A brief explanation of Table 5 is appended below.

Considering the intangibles to determine the possibility of a surprise attack by Hamas on Israel on October 7, 2023, one can see that from Hamas's perspective, such an attack was always desirable because the resistance group was weary of the fact that more and more Islamic states were building relationships with Israel, and the demand for the Two-State solution was not even considered at any level. However, from the Palestinian state's perspective, the Hamas actions were highly undesirable, because they provided a reason to raze Gaza to the ground and undertake the genocide of the Palestinians.

From Hamas's perspective, the attack on Israeli territory and taking a few hostages to bargain on its demands may have been preferable, but it certainly was not a priority of the Palestinian people and Palestinian Authority headed by Mahmoud Abbas of the Palestine Liberation Organization (PLO). Hamas assumed that their action would receive outright support from all the Muslim countries. However, their assumption proved faulty, and barring a few statements, no worthwhile support came from any of the Muslim countries. However, Hamas had the political will to undertake the October 7, 2023,

**Table 5:** Hamas Attacks on Israel on P2 (Possibility-Probability) Model

|  | Desirability | Preferability | Favorability | Political Will |
|---|---|---|---|---|
| Possibility | From Hamas's perspective, such an attack was always desirable to keep the issue of a Two-State solution alive. | From Hamas's perspective, the attack on Israeli territory and taking hostages to bargain on its demands may have been preferable, but it certainly was not a priority of the Palestinian state. | Hamas assumed that their action would receive outright support from all the Muslim countries. | Hamas had the political will to undertake the October 7 action without due consideration of Israel and the Western world's reaction. |
|  | Doability | Capacity | Sustainability | Exit Strategy |
| Probability | If the tangible military elements are considered, an attack on Israel by Hamas was not doable. | Hamas could not absorb Israel's response which is beyond proportion. | Hamas could not sustain its offensive and its expectations that other Muslim states would join in its just war proved fatal. | Hamas did not have an exit strategy. It was based on wrong assumptions. |

action without due consideration of Israel and the Western world's reaction. The price is now being paid by the poor non-combatant Palestinians.

To determine the probabilities of Hamas's actions of October 7, 2023, the tangible military elements are considered, and one can conclude that an attack on Israel by Hamas was not doable primarily because it lacked capability against a much bigger and stronger adversary. Moreover, Hamas could not absorb Israel's response which is beyond proportion, and hence the genocide of poor Palestinians is continuing without any break under the guise of self-defense, fully supported by the US and Western allies.

Due to capability and capacity issues, Hamas could not sustain its offensive and its expectations that other Muslim states would join in its just war was faulty and hence proved fatal. Consequently, Hamas did not have an exit strategy because the entire plan was based on wrong assumptions and perhaps on suicidal lines, and that is what is exactly happening. While the whole world is calling upon Israel to stop the genocide of the Palestinian people, including

Table 6: Israel's Response to D2 (Diplomacy-Deterrence) Model

|  | Diplomacy | Deterrence |
|---|---|---|
| Israel | Israel was able to convince the US-led Western Bloc that it was attacked by Hamas unjustly and its citizens were taken hostage in an act of terrorism. | Israel's military failed to deter Hamas and therefore Hamas was able to achieve the surprise in its initial actions. |
| Hamas | Hamas failed to convince even the Muslim countries that its initial acts were legitimate. | Hamas was able to surprise initially but it does not have a sustainable deterrent value of its own. |
| US | The US engaged in negative diplomacy and kept on supporting Israel in its all-out offensive instead of making any worthwhile diplomatic effort to avert an impending genocide of the Palestinian people. | The US was not deterred by the worldwide anger for its all-out support of Israeli atrocities in the name of self-defense. |
| The UN | The UN's effort for a ceasefire remained fruitless even when its members were killed by Israeli bombings. | The UN has zero deterrent value when it comes to any actions against the US and Israel. |
| Organization of Islamic Countries (OIC) | OIC made no worthwhile effort to enforce a ceasefire. Only Qatar was successful in its effort to get through a humanitarian pause. | OIC does not carry any deterrent value, particularly against Israel and the US. |

the International Court of Justice (ICJ), Israel is just not letting off any pressure because it has the unwavering support of the US-led Western world.

A brief explanation of Table 6 is appended below.

In the domain of diplomacy, Israel was able to convince the US-led Western Bloc that it was attacked by Hamas unjustly, and its citizens were taken hostage in an act of terrorism, and it has the right to defend itself and take revenge to eliminate Hamas.

On the other hand, Hamas failed to convince even the Muslim countries that its initial acts were legitimate and therefore were not supported. Later, once Israel committed genocide of the Palestinian people, the world started to speak for them but not for the Hamas.

The US engaged in negative diplomacy and kept on supporting Israel in its all-out offensive instead of making any worthwhile diplomatic effort to avert an impending genocide of the Palestinian people. On each occasion in the UNSC, the US vetoed the ceasefire resolution.

The UN's effort for a ceasefire remained fruitless even when its members were killed by Israeli bombings. The UN remains a toothless organization when it comes to supporting a weaker power. Western countries have even withdrawn funding to UNRWA under Israeli pressure, but the UN remains ineffective.

Israel's military failed to deter Hamas and therefore Hamas was able to achieve the surprise in its initial actions. Israel has still not been able to re-establish deterrence and Hamas, Hezbollah, and Houthis continue to fire rockets and drones on the Israeli territory.

Hamas was able to surprise initially but it does not have a sustainable deterrent value of its own or with its like-minded groups in the region to deter Israel from carrying out the genocide of the Palestinian people in its out-of-proportion revenge that has been largely criticized by people around the world except for a few governments like the US and UK.

Likewise, the US was not deterred by the worldwide anger for its all-out support of Israeli atrocities in the name of self-defense. Despite huge protests by the people across the US, the Biden Administration remains part of Israeli atrocities on the Palestinian people.

The UN remains toothless and has zero deterrent value when it comes to any actions against the US and Israel. Its relief workers have been killed in Israeli bombings, but it has no punitive authority to control Israelis from undertaking the genocide of the Palestinians. Similarly, OIC also remains a symbolic organization and does not carry any deterrent value, particularly against Israel and the US.

Another conflict selected to discuss in this book on P2 and D2 Models is the KSA-led Blockade of the State of Qatar (2017–2020). This was the most uncalled-for and perhaps the most useless conflict of the 21$^{st}$ century that occurred in a relatively peaceful Gulf sub-region of the otherwise conflict-ridden Middle East. Even after the formal conclusion of the conflict, people are investigating the causes and the purpose of the blockade of a much smaller and brotherly Muslim neighbor.

**Table 7:** KSA-led Blockade of Qatar on P2 (Possibility-Probability) Model

|             | Desirability | Preferability | Favorability | Political Will |
|-------------|--------------|---------------|--------------|----------------|
| Possibility | Highly Desirable from the KSA-led quartet who was weary of Qatar's rising stature. | From the KSA-led perspective, the Blockade of Qatar was preferred over an outright invasion. | KSA-led quartet assumed that they could win the favorability of the Muslim states and the US-led Western world due to their politico-economic stature. | The KSA-led quartet was motivated by a strong political will to reduce Qatar to its size. |
|             | Doability    | Capacity      | Sustainability | Exit Strategy |
| Probability | If the tangible military elements are considered, the Blockade of Qatar was doable by the initiators. | The KSA-led quartet had the military and economic capacity to enforce a Blockade on a tiny Gulf state, Qatar. | The KSA-led quartet had the military, economic, and political will to sustain their act of Blockade. | The KSA-led quartet did not have an Exit Strategy, because they assumed that Qatar would succumb to pressure. |

An evaluation of P2 is shown in Table 7, whereas Table 8 shows the analysis of D2.

A brief explanation of Table 7 is appended below.

From the perspective of the KSA-led quartet, it was highly desirable to enforce a politico-economic blockade of Qatar because the Saudis and Emiratis were weary of Qatar's rising stature. The bigger neighbors viewed Qatar as too independent in its foreign policy decisions and playing the role of a regional peacemaker by facilitating peace talks in conflict zones.

On the scale of preferability, and the KSA-led quartet's perspective, the Blockade of Qatar was a preferred option over an outright invasion, even though a ground invasion of the tiny Gulf neighbor was planned as outlined by Qatar's Defense Minister in his interview with Washington Post.[5]

In the contemporary international order, it is important to consider both public opinion and the state's opinion. The KSA-led quartet assumed that they could win the favorability of the Muslim states and the US-led Western world due to their politico-economic stature. However, they did not visualize or did not care for a much smaller brotherly neighbor which also had a good rapport and always showed responsible behavior in its relations with other states. Therefore, it was no surprise that many of the nations supported Qatar and criticized the KSA-led quartet for being aggressive against a much smaller neighbor.

The KSA-led quartet was motivated by a strong political will to reduce Qatar to its size, and therefore, all four nations: Saudi Arabia, UAE, Bahrain, and Egypt, felt very strongly about going ahead with the Blockade of Qatar.

On the other hand, if the tangible military elements are considered to determine the probability of the Blockade of Qatar, it was certainly doable by the initiators. The combined military capabilities of the four countries could easily enforce the blockade for an unlimited period to bring Qatar to terms, as per their perspectives. Similarly, the KSA-led quartet had the military and economic capacity to enforce a blockade on a much weaker State of Qatar and sustain it for an unlimited period. Consequently, the blockade continued for well over three years.

The KSA-led quartet did not have an Exit Strategy; perhaps they assumed that Qatar would succumb to pressure. However, Qatar's leadership refused to budge from its stated position and remained defiant to the charges of illegal support to terror groups. Qatar continued to call for a peaceful resolution of the dispute and relied more on its allies through diplomacy and a robust economy. The period of blockade (June 2017–December 2022) was very crucial because Qatar was preparing to host FIFA-2022 for which massive infrastructure projects were in full swing when the blockade was imposed. However, Qatar showed exemplary resilience and diplomatic skills to maintain the ongoing work related to FIFA-2022 projects and ended up organizing the best-ever mega event in history. Consequently, by that time the blockade had been lifted and relations between the Gulf nations had returned to normal.

A brief explanation of Table 8 is appended below.

Qatar's positive diplomacy played a pivotal role in averting a war in the Gulf sub-region. As stated earlier, at least one of the essential tools: diplomacy or deterrence, must work to avert a war. In this case, diplomacy worked to its true sense and hence was able to deny any space to the initiators to carry out kinetic operations even though it had been planned. However, the KSA-led quartet's negative diplomacy placed the entire region on the edge of wider conflict. Moreover, the UN and all other international institutions were supportive of Qatar and called for the lifting of the Blockade. The US played a

Table 8: Qatar's Response to D2 (Diplomacy-Deterrence) Model

|  | Diplomacy | Deterrence |
|---|---|---|
| **Qatar** | Qatar's positive diplomacy played a pivotal role in averting a war in the Gulf sub-region. | Qatar did not have the military strength to deter the initiators but made full use of its alliances, particularly Turkey. |
| **KSA-led Quartet** | KSA-led quartet's negative diplomacy placed the entire region on the edge of a wider conflict. | Despite being 10 times larger in military strength, initiators failed to deter Qatar from its principled stance. |
| **The UN** | The UN and all other international institutions were supportive of Qatar and called for the lifting of the Blockade. | The UN did not deter the aggressors but put its weight behind Qatar. |
| **US** | The US played a positive diplomatic role in the entire period of conflict. | The US Air Base at Al Udeid in Qatar may have acted as a deterrent to put a hold on the ground invasion of Qatar. |
| **EU** | The EU played a positive diplomatic role in the entire period of conflict. | The EU did not deter the aggressors but put its weight behind Qatar. |
| **Other Muslim States** | Kuwait, Turkey, and Iran played a positive diplomatic role in containing the conflict. | The presence of Turkish troops may have deterred the initiators from launching an invasion of Qatar. |

positive diplomatic role in the entire period of conflict. Kuwait, Turkey, and Iran played a positive diplomatic role in containing the conflict.

On the scale of deterrence, Qatar did not have the military strength to deter the initiators but made full use of its alliances, particularly Turkey. Despite being 10 times larger in military strength, initiators failed to deter Qatar from its principled stance. Whereas the UN could not deter the aggressors but put its weight behind Qatar. Perhaps, the US Air Base at Al Udeid in Qatar may have acted as a deterrent to put a hold on the ground invasion of Qatar. Similarly, the EU did not deter the aggressors but put its weight behind Qatar. However, the presence of Turkish troops in Qatar as part of a strategic agreement on security may have deterred the initiators from launching an invasion of Qatar.

A detailed analysis of these three conflicts and wars reinforces the author's views that if both diplomacy and deterrence are working, the relationship between the states would be stable. However, if at least one is working, the war can be averted, but if none is working, there will be a high probability of a violent conflict. Interestingly both diplomacy and deterrence can be re-established even during crises, conflicts, or after the outbreak of war. Therefore, the efforts must continue to deny the aggressors any space to initiate physical violence because it cannot be controlled thereafter.

## Interdependence of Diplomacy and Deterrence

The above discussion on P2 and D2 aptly proves that these two tools that each state has or may have depending upon its strengths and weaknesses, are interdependent and inseparable, to achieve the desired peace, stability, and security between the states bilaterally or in multilateral settings. This author opines that if at least one is working, there is a medium probability that military engagement between the states with protracted conflicts could be averted. However, if both tools deliver the desired results, the two states can have a period of relative peace, stability, and security during which they can progress on the path of conflict resolution from a period of conflict management.

On the other hand, if none of these tools is working, there is a high probability that a violent conflict will be unavoidable. However, the beauty of these two tools that each state has lies in the interdependence and inseparability of the two in all situations: before, during, and after the wars and conflicts. Because both these tools can re-establish themselves either singly or in combination. For instance, diplomacy never sleeps and remains active in all situations looking to make possible the least probable. At the height of tension between the two states, diplomacy continues to strive for a way out to avert a military engagement, and once the war has started, it aims for an early ceasefire to contain the loss of men and material. Exceptions are always there, and one can see that at present also where Israel continues to carry out the genocide of the poor Palestinians with the US giving full coverage at the UNSC. Likewise, Russia continues to advance deep into Ukrainian territory with China fully supporting it.

On the other hand, deterrence also re-establishes itself once the escalation ladder ascends and causes alarm bells in the corridors of world powers. For instance, on each occasion when the limited wars broke out between the two nuclear neighbors in South Asia: India and Pakistan, it was the US that intervened with all its might and resources to contain the conflict before any of the two even resorted to nuclear posturing. It is in this context this author opines that diplomacy and deterrence can still manage the wars and conflicts between equal military powers or near equal military powers but the wars between UMPs remain at large.

## Conclusion

To conclude this chapter, it would be prudent to highlight the results of the analysis carried out on different academic tools and models to determine the efficacy of diplomacy and deterrence as essential elements to attain, maintain, and sustain peace, stability, and security in the region and beyond. In each war and conflict, one can find that either the military action was not doable or even if it was doable, it was not preferable. Moreover, in contemporary times, it is extremely difficult to convince other regional and international institutions about the necessity of war, therefore, in many of the cases it is seen that the hostile actions did not have global favorability for initiators acts. Israel is an exception which gets instant approval for its acts of genocide and crimes against humanity by the US and its Western allies.

However, diplomacy without the organic support of a strong hard power was able to save the day for Qatar against a much stronger regional group primarily because the hostile acts of the neighboring states did not get a favorable response by the regional or international institutions. Therefore, for smaller nations particularly, the hybrid employment of diplomacy and deterrence must be perhaps the only way to survive in this anarchic international system that rides on the precepts of realism. Qatar has proven this argument through the skillful employment of all its resources in a hybrid manner from the moment the blockade was imposed till it was finally lifted and that too without conceding to any of the demands of the blockading countries. One can argue that Qatar is a rich country with the highest per capita income in the world and therefore it managed and survived the hostile actions of the regional partners. However, this author opines that it was not the money alone that saved Qatar from an imminent invasion by the KSA-led quartet, but the leadership, people, and skillful employment of diplomacy well supported by the deterrent value gathered through alliance partners.

The states are not equal in size, population, resources, and geographical features. However, they are blessed with several multipliers that need to be deployed in a hybrid manner to accumulate and improve the deterrent value to survive in the prevalent international system. It is up to each state to recognize its strengths and weaknesses and blend diplomacy and deterrence in a hybrid manner to attain, maintain, and sustain peace, stability, and security in the region and beyond.

## Notes

1 David Carter, Deterrence, https://openoregon.pressbooks.pub/ccj230/chapter/8-3-deterrence/ (accessed August 5, 2023). "It begins with a brief intellectual history of deterrence theory in the work of Cesare Beccaria and Jeremy Bentham, two Enlightenment philosophers who created the conceptual foundation for later deterrence and rational choice theory."
2 Ijaz ul Haq, "Zia Threatened Rajiv with Nukes on a Trip to India," *The News*, August 17, 2016, https://www.thenews.com.pk/print/143092-Zia-threatened-Rajiv-with-nukes-on-trip-to-India (accessed August 5, 2023).
3 The Shanghai Cooperation Organization, January 9, 2017, https://eng.sectsco.org/20170109/192193.html (accessed January 30, 2024).
4 Ibid.
5 Lally Weymouth, "Qatar to Saudi Arabia: Quit Trying to Overthrow Our Government," *The Washington Post*, February 2, 2018, https://gulfif.org/qatar-to-saudi-arabia-quit-trying-to-overthrow-our-government/ (accessed November 21, 2023).

# CONCLUSION

The title of the book is indicative of the significance of the two terms or tools the states have, diplomacy and deterrence, to protect and promote their interests and ensure their territorial integrity and sovereignty. However, the efficacy of the two, diplomacy and deterrence, is highly dependent on the skillful employment of diplomacy and the effective deployment of the deterrent value each state may have depending on its capacity to project its power. Since the two tools, diplomacy, and deterrence, have nearly similar objectives, therefore, they must be employed in a hybrid manner either concurrently or sequentially. There is little doubt that given the objectives in the respective domains, diplomacy and deterrence, will have to complement each other to ensure that the other one delivers. For instance, an imminent war can be averted through proactive and intense diplomacy even if the deterrence has failed, however, the probability of a military engagement will increase manifolds if both diplomacy and fail to deliver. Therefore, it is necessary that at least one must deliver to avoid wars and conflicts, however, to attain, maintain, and sustain peace, stability, and security, both diplomacy and deterrence will have to deliver. This author opines that the hybrid employment of diplomacy and deterrence may be the most suitable manner to achieve the desired results.

The purpose of this book is to reemphasize the need for hybrid employment of blended diplomacy and deterrence to attain, maintain, and sustain peace, stability, and security within the region and beyond. Several conflict-ridden regions need a sustainable effort to achieve peace and stability because the unnecessary wars and conflicts have those regions and states left poor with the least number of livable amenities. Most notable among these are South Asia, Africa, and the Middle East where millions of lives have been lost during territorial wars, civil wars, and fighting for independence following foreign occupation. The 21$^{st}$ century wars have been more killing because most wars have been fought between the UMPs.

Recounting the two essential tools titled and discussed in the book, diplomacy, and deterrence, one can count on the two to achieve the desired objectives of peace, stability, and security. While this may sound too idealistic it is certainly doable because mankind is faced with far greater challenges than the territorial disputes in the 21$^{st}$ century. International institutions are still grappling with the impact of pandemics while it is still not over, the food and energy crises due to the ongoing Russia-Ukraine war are causing high inflation due to supply chain management issues. On the other hand, Israel is committing genocide of the unarmed Palestinians with the fullest support of the US and its Western allies.

Briefly, diplomacy always remains at work on all its avenues and states are never sure which effort would be successful on which front, therefore, the states that discontinue diplomatic relations with adversaries are the net losers. Whereas the states that continue to knock on each door always emerge victorious in the prevalent international system which is based on the realist paradigm.

Interestingly, in the domain of peace and conflict, it is the international and regional diplomacy that can help the relatively smaller states. However, on other fronts, bilateral diplomatic efforts can also bring favorable results. When Qatar was faced with an existential threat, its resistance was led by proactive diplomacy on all fronts. Qatar deployed its diplomatic efforts on all available avenues: external relations, defense diplomacy, economic diplomacy, sports diplomacy, and legal options. Qatar fought back vigorously on all fronts against a much bigger alliance that had imposed an illegal, unjust, and uncalled-for blockade that was aimed at choking the small peninsular state.

On the other hand, Ukraine, a relatively bigger European state that had the full support of the NATO countries failed to avoid a war against its much bigger and historical ally. Russia had declared Ukraine as its red line fearing that if the country joins NATO, it would be faced with an existential threat. However, Ukraine did not make any diplomatic effort to allay the concerns of Russia. Even when the war was imminent, neither Ukraine nor any of its NATO supporters made any effort to prevent war instead they provided financial and material support to the country to fight against a much bigger opponent. Consequently, Ukraine started to lose territory and lives even with considerable support from a militarily strong ally, NATO.

Likewise, the deterrence regime may have certain avenues, as discussed in Chapter 5, it is believed that deterrence is not a given and needs to be revisited. According to Michael Keane: "The prevention or inhibition of action brought about by fear of the consequences. Deterrence is a state of mind brought about by the existence of a credible threat of unacceptable counteraction. It assumes and requires rational decision-makers."[1]

In modern times the concept, and definitions, draw reference to the birth of nuclear weapons in 1945. Bernard Brodie, the strategist of nuclear deterrence theory, was of the view that "if aggressor feared retaliation in kind, he would not attack."[2] Explaining further, Brodie wrote, "Thus far the chief purpose of our military establishment has been to win wars. From now on its chief purpose must be to avert them."[3] However, deterrence is not a given; it is to be acquired, and it is to be accomplished through certain measures, and actions. Moreover, it is relative, and not across the board. Furthermore, neither it is permanent, nor guaranteed, especially when the two nuclear neighbors have a history of wars, conflicts, and crises at regular intervals, without embracing conflict resolution mechanisms, and just managing them from the brink.

However, Afghans could not be deterred and emerged victorious after two decades of destruction by the US-led Western alliances. Yemeni resistance groups could not be deterred by the KSA-led alliances even as the conflict entered the eighth year. Yemen is faced with famine and the worst form of humanitarian disaster.

The situation in South Asia with regards to nuclear equation appears to be entirely different and quite strange. India and Pakistan are de facto nuclear states since May 1998 when India carried out its second wave of nuclear tests after a gap of nearly 24 years. India managed to achieve the surprise, but Pakistan had to face the wrath of Indian action. The international community launched an assertive campaign to refrain Pakistan from carrying out its nuclear tests to even with India. But Pakistan refused to compromise on its security and carried out five nuclear explosions on 28 May 1998, followed by another two days later. Pakistan only tested its capability in response to Indian tests within three weeks and thus two South Asian rivals declared themselves nuclear states. Pakistan's nuclear tests, in response to that of the Indians, perhaps reduced the strategic imbalance in the region but placed immense responsibility on its leadership. Because, the western world, particularly the US considers South Asia a dangerous place because of frequent wars, conflicts and crises between India and Pakistan over the disputed territories of J&K. US and its allies remain overly concerned about the nuclear safety and security issues, particularly for Pakistan, although Pakistan carries an excellent record of nuclear safety and security.

To address the concerns of the safety and security of its nuclear assets and installations, Pakistan quickly moved to announce an apt nuclear policy, designed a comprehensive nuclear doctrine and established a reliable command, control, communication, and intelligence structure. Pakistan also ensured and incorporated stringent safety measures to avert its inadvertent and unauthorized use.

The tradition of deterrence was well understood as it meant the dissuasion of hostile activities by a country against the other for the fear of unbreakable consequences, and both the superpowers accepted the concept in its essence and did not challenge each other directly militarily even when the era of the new cold war began with Soviet invasion of Afghanistan in 1979. Moreover, the two superpowers did not have a direct territorial dispute. The ideological differences lay in their systems of economy, and power politics to have more countries under their direct influence.

Whereas in the South Asian contest, both India and Pakistan are enduring one of the most complex disputes over J&K, which has an ideological, territorial strategic, and economic dimension. They also have other territorial disputes on Siachen and Sir Creek. Water dispute is another aspect that may lead to survival issues in the years to come. In an environment of protracted conflicts, and active disputes, the introduction of nuclear dimension on both sides is seen as a stabilizing factor, at least in avoidance of an all-out conventional war. However, limited military engagements, both on the ground and in the air, have continued at regular intervals. If the sole purpose of acquiring nuclear weapons was to avoid a conventional war, then it has served the purpose until now and perhaps may serve in future also. India seems to be striving to increase the conventional asymmetry through the massive induction of modern weapons systems in its armed forces under the BECA with the US. Also, India does not consider it appropriate to discuss any of the outstanding disputes toward its logical resolution, because the maintenance of the status quo affords it time to concentrate on strengthening and modernizing its armed forces and economy. Pakistan is missing the trick. Its economy is in dire state, and it can hardly afford the much-needed modernization of its armed forces, hence relying on its existing inventory, complemented by the nuclear card.

Since the overt nuclearization of South Asia in May 1998, India and Pakistan have had several limited wars, conflicts, and crises, which were declared as dangerous and culminated only with the active intervention of the US.

True deterrence should be able to prevent adversaries from planning and organizing, acts of violence and war of any kind due to the fear of such consequences that it could ill afford. The meaning of deterrence needs to be redefined in the changed paradigm. The traditional meaning and concept of deterrence may have worked between the Cold War rivals at that time, but it needs a serious review by the academics and the practitioners alike, to avoid the next war.

To conclude, this author is of the view that neither diplomacy nor deterrence alone can guarantee peace, stability, and security. Therefore, it is reemphasized that blending these two tools in a hybrid manner is essentially required to attain, maintain, and sustain peace, stability, and security in any region and beyond. Unfortunately, the same had been missing in several countries in the conflict-ridden regions: South Asia, the Middle East, Europe, and now Africa, which is on the verge of a full-fledged war over Niger, at the time of this submission.

Both diplomacy and deterrence are powerful tools the states have and if employed effectively in a hybrid manner concurrently or sequentially, will help in attaining, maintaining, and sustaining peace, stability, and security in the region and beyond. In recent times, Qatar has proved the efficacy of this argument positively that an imminent war can be averted and won without firing a bullet. On the other hand, Ukraine is facing disastrous consequences of an ongoing war against a relatively bigger and stronger neighbor primarily because it did not employ the available tools, diplomacy, and deterrence, in a manner that could convince Russia not to attack.

To conclude, this author opines that to survive in the present anarchic international system, states must strive to improve their deterrent value either organically or through strategic agreements with stronger allies and deploy positive diplomacy in a hybrid manner to attain, maintain, and sustain peace, stability, and security in the region and beyond. The purpose of repeating this argument throughout this book was to reiterate the need to avoid wars and conflicts primarily because humanity is faced with existential threats by many other challenges like pandemics, climate changes, food shortages, energy deficiencies, cyber warfare, digital divide, and human displacements due to extensive use of gun powder by the US-led allies against the UMPs, and Israel against the Palestinians. Academics and practitioners must strive to find ways and means to avert the next war before the ongoing wars in the Middle East, South Asia, and Europe expand their wings to engulf the nearby regions.

## Notes

1 Stephen Kuper, "Strategic Deterrence: More Than Just Nukes," *Geopolitica & Policy*, October 30, 2018, https://www.defenceconnect.com.au/key-enablers/3079-strategic-deterrence-more-than-just-nukes (accessed August 5, 2023).
2 Bernard Brodie, *The Absolute Weapon: Atomic Power and the World Order* (Institute of International, Studies, Yale University, 1946). Accessed November 15, 2013.
3 Bernard Brodie, *The Atomic Bomb and American Security*, Occasional Paper no. 18 (Yale Institute of International Studies, 1945). See also an expanded version of this paper in Bernard Brodie, *The Absolute Weapon* (New York: Harcourt, Brace, and Company, 1946).

# BIBLIOGRAPHY

## Primary Sources

## Treaties, Agreements, Conventions, Declarations and Reports

1. Agreement for Bringing Peace to Afghanistan between the Islamic Emirate of Afghanistan which is not recognized by the United States as a state and is known as the Taliban and the United States of America. February 29, 2020.
2. *Constitution of India*.
3. *Congressional Research Service Report.* March 25, 2021.
4. Durand Line Agreement. *Agreement between Amir Abdur Rahman Khan, G. C. S. I., and Sir Henry Mortimer Durand, K. C. I. E., C. S. I.* November 12, 1893.
5. Ebrahim, Zofeen T. *Pakistan Green Again.* The UNESCO Courier, 2019–2023.
6. SIGAR, Quarterly Report to the United States Congress. April 30, 2020.
7. *The Simla Agreement* was signed between India and Pakistan. July 2, 1972.
8. The World Bank Report. *The Potential of Intra-regional Trade for South Asia.* May 2016.
9. *UNDP Human Development Report.* 2020.
10. Geneva Convention relative to the Treatment of Prisoners of War. Adopted on August 12, 1949.
11. Nathan Williams reports for BBC on October 7, 2022, "Ukraine War: Biden Says Nuclear Risk Highest Since 1962 Cuban Missile Crisis of 1962."

12. The Boundary Agreement between China and Pakistan. July 27, 1963.
13. The Lahore Declaration was signed by the Prime Ministers of India and Pakistan on 21 February 1999 in Lahore.
14. "The Saudi Intervention in Yemen: Struggling for Status." *Insight Turkey* 20, no. 2 (Spring 2018).
15. Aamoth, Doug. "First Smartphone Turns 20: Fun Facts about Simon." *TIME*. August 18, 2014.
16. Indian Chronicles: Deep Dive into a 15–Year-Old Operation Targeting the EU and the UN to Serve Indian Interests. 2020.
17. Edited extract from *Post-Cold War Conflict Deterrence*. Naval Studies Board, National Research Council, National Academy of Sciences. 1997.
18. Jopling, Lord. "Countering Russia's Hybrid Threats: An Update." Draft Special Report, NATO Parliamentary Assembly. 2018.

## Journals, Monographs, Papers

1. Abbasi, Rizwana. "Enduring India-Pakistan Rivalry: Prospects for Conflict Resolution." *Regional Studies* XXXIII, no. 3 (Summer 2015).
2. Ahmad, Shamshad. *Shifting Dynamics and Emerging Power Equilibrium in South and Central Asia around Post-2014*. Islamabad-Pakistan: Strategic Vision Institute, 2014.
3. Ahmad, Shamshad. "The Nuclear Subcontinent: Bringing Stability to South Asia." *Foreign Affairs* 78, no. 4 (July/August 1999).
4. Ahmed, Samina, and Sahni, Varun. *Freezing the Fighting: Military Disengagement on the Siachen Glacier*. Occasional Paper-1. Springfield, VA 22161: Cooperative Monitoring Centre, 1998.
5. Ayoob, Mohammad. "Security for South Asia: Searching for Key-Variable." *Newsletter of Regional Studies (Colombo)* 3, no. 4 (1997).
6. Basrur, Rajesh M. "International Relations Theory and Minimum Deterrence." *India Review* 4, no. 2 (April 2005).
7. Biswas, Asit K. "Indus Water Treaty: The Negotiating Process." *Water International* 17 (1992).
8. Brodie, Bernard. "Nuclear Weapons: Strategic or Tactical." *Foreign Affairs* (January 1954).
9. Brodie, Bernard. *The Atomic Bomb and American Security*. Occasional Paper no. 18. Baltimore, Maryland, USA 21218: Yale Institute of International Studies, 1945.
10. Burgess, G., and H. Burgess, ed. "Security." *Beyond Intractability*. Conflict Research Consortium. Colorado, Boulder: University of Colorado, 2003.
11. Cheema, Pervaiz Iqbal. "Significance of Pakistan-China Border Agreement of 1963." *Pakistan Horizon* 39 (1986).
12. Dalrymple, William. "The Great Divide: The Violent Legacy of Indian Partition." *The New Yorker*, June 2015.
13. Dubey, Muchkund. *Culture of Peace in Central South Asia*. Islamabad: Margalla Press, 1995.

14. Evera, Stephen Van. "Offense, Defense, and the Causes of War." *International Security* 22, no. 4 (Spring 1998).
15. Hagerty, Devin T. "Nuclear Deterrence in South Asia: The 1990 Indo-Pak Crisis." *International Security* 20, no. 3 (Winter 1995–1996).
16. Ghani, Usman. "Nuclear Weapons in India-Pakistan Crisis." *IPRI Journal* XII, no. 2 (Summer 2012): 137-145.
17. Husain, Ishrat, and Muhammad Ather Elahi. *The Future of Afghanistan-Pakistan Trade Relations*. United States Institute of Peace. Washington, DC, 2015.
18. Jervis, Robert. "Realism, Neoliberalism, and Cooperation; Understanding the Debate." *International Security* 31, no. 4 (Summer 1999).
19. Jones, Rodney W. *India's Strategic Culture*. Report written for U.S. Defense Threat Reduction Agency, Comparative Strategic Cultures Curriculum, 2006.
20. Joshi, Shashank. "Pakistan's Tactical Nuclear Nightmare: Deja Vu?" *The Washington Quarterly* 36, no. 3 (Summer 2013).
21. Karl, David J. "Proliferation Optimism and Pessimism Revisited." *Journal of Strategic Studies* 34, no. 4 (August 2011).
22. Kaushiva, Pradeep. *The Sir Creek Imbroglio*. New Delhi: National Maritime Foundation, 2013.
23. Khan, Aarish U. "Siachen Glacier: Getting Past the Deadlock." *Institute of Regional Studies* XXXI, no. 5 (May 2012).
24. Khan, Rashid Ahmad. "Sir Creek: The Origins and Development of the Dispute between India and Pakistan." *IPRI Journal (Islamabad)*, no. 2 (Summer 2007): 1-13.
25. Khan, Zafar. *Cold Start Doctrine: The Conventional Challenge to South Asian Stability*. London: Routledge, Contemporary Security Policy, 2012.
26. Khan, Zulfqar, and Rizwana Abbasi. "Regional-Centric Deterrence: Reassessing Its Efficacy for South Asia." *The Korean Journal of Defense Analysis*, no. 4 (December 2013).
27. Klass, R. T. "The Great Game Revisited." *National Review* 31, no. 43 (October 1979).
28. Kugelman, Michael, and Robert M. Hathaway (ed.). *Pakistan-India Trade: What Needs to Be Done? What Does It Matter?* Ijaz Nabi, Pakistan's Trade with India: Thinking Strategically. Washington, DC.: The Wilson Center, 2013. Washington, DC.
29. Maizland, Lindsay, and Eleanor Albert. *What Is ASEAN?* Council on Foreign Relations. New York, USA, 2021.
30. Malik, Zaman. "Propaganda and Psychological Subversion." *Defence Journal (Islamabad)* (September 2002).
31. Mearsheimer, John J. "The False Promise of International Institutions." *International Security* 19, no. 3 (1995).
32. Narang, Vipin. "Five Myths about India's Nuclear Policy." *The Washington Quarterly* (Summer 2013).
33. Noorani A.G. "The Siachen Impasse." *Frontline* 19, no. 23 (November 2002).
34. Nosheen and Toheeda Begum. "Indus Water Treaty & Emergency Water Issues." *Abasyn Journal of Social Sciences* 4, no. 2 (2012).
35. Posen, Barry. "The Security Dilemma and Ethnic Conflict." *Survival* 35, no. 1 (Spring 1993).
36. Rothschild, Emma. "What Is Security." *Daedalus* 24, no. 3 (Summer 1995).

37. Ruggie, J. "What Makes the World Hang Together? Neo-utilitarianism and the Social Constructivist Challenge." *International Organization* 52, no. 4 (Autumn 1998).
38. Shamsi, Zia Ul Haque. "Strategic Neglect of Sun Tzu's Precepts: A Case Study of Kargil Conflict." *NDU Journal* XXVII (2013): 121–138.
39. Shamsi, Zia Ul Haque. "Realism Impedes the Process of Arms Control and Disarmament: It's Time to Change the Theory and Strategy" *SunText Review of Arts & Social Sciences* 4, no. 3 (December 2023): 165.
40. Shamsi, Zia Ul Haque. "Significance of Non-Traditional Dimensions of Security: Understanding Pakistan's Predicaments." *IJCISS* 2, no. 4 (December 2023).
41. Shamsi, Zia Ul Haque. "Efficacy of Social Media in Wars and Conflict: Brief Review of Russia-Ukraine War." *CARC Research in Social Sciences* 2, no. 4 (December 2023): 202–207.
42. Shamsi, Zia Ul Haque. "Evaluating the Potential of Cultural Diplomacy as 'A Weapon of Enduring Peace in the Gulf Region.'" *Pakistan Journal of Humanities and Social Sciences* 11, no. 4 (2023): 4280–4287.
43. Shamsi, Zia Ul Haque. "Massive Retaliation Against Unequal Military Powers (UMPs)." *International Journal of Contemporary Issues in Social Sciences* 2, no. 3 (September 2023).
44. Shamsi, Zia Ul Haque. "Why Do Nations War: Ideology, Territory, Power and Security in?" *International Journal of Contemporary Issues in Social Sciences* 2, no. 4 (December 2023): 878–888.
45. Shamsi, Zia Ul Haque. "Introducing Realizm." *Progressive Research Journal of Arts and Humanities (PRJAH)* 3, no. 2 (2022): 1–13.
46. Shamsi, Zia Ul Haque. "Hybrid Warfare and Its Nuances: A Case Study from South Asia, Joint Article with Dr. Farah Naz." *IPRI Journal* XXII, no. 1 (2022): 25–43.
47. Shamsi, Zia Ul Haque. "Deterrence and Diplomacy: Investigating India's Motives Behind Conflict Deferment and Pakistan's Endeavors at Conflict Resolution." *CISS Insight, Journal of Strategic Studies* 10, no. 2 (2022).
48. Shamsi, Zia Ul Haque. "Impermanence of Deterrence Regime: A Cause of Tactical Instability in South Asia." *Journal of Aerospace & Security Studies* 1 (2022): 85–100.
49. Shamsi, Zia Ul Haque. "Theory of Fear and Tear: A Consequence of Deterrence Failure." *Journal of Xi'an Shiyou University, Natural Science Edition* 20, no. 1 (January 2024): 75–87.
50. Shamsi, Zia Ul Haque, "Introducing the Framework Model for the Evaluation of Deterrent Value of States," NUST *Journal of International Peace & Stability*, 2024, Vol. 7(2) Pages 1-15, njips.nust.edu.pk DOI: http://doi.org/10.37540/njips.v7i2.170.
51. Swantron, Niklas L.P., and Mikael S. Weismann. *Conflict, Conflict Prevention, Conflict Management, and Beyond: A Conceptual Exploration*. Concept paper published by the Central Asia-Caucasus Institute & Silk Road Studies Program, Sweden, 2005.
52. Taliaferro, Jeffrey W. "Security-Seeking Under Anarchy: Defensive Realism Reconsidered." *International Security* 25, no. 3 (Winter 2000–2001).
53. Tellis, Ashley J., C. Christine Fair, and Jamison Jo Medby. *Limited Conflicts under the Nuclear Umbrella: Indian and Pakistani Lessons from the Kargil Conflict*. Santa Monica, CA: Rand, 2001.
54. Waltz, Kenneth. *Spread of Nuclear Weapons: More May Better*. Adelphi Papers, no. 171. London: International Institute for Strategic Studies, 1981.

55. Waltz, Kenneth N. "Nuclear Myths and Political Realities." *American Political Science Review* 84, no. 3 (September 1990).
56. Walt, Stephen M. "International Relations: One World, Many Theories." *Foreign Policy*, no. 110, Special Edition: Frontiers of Knowledge (Spring, 1998): 29-32, 34-46.
57. Wen, Wang, and Chen Xiaochen. "Who Supports China in the South China Sea and Why?" *The Diplomat*, July 2016.
58. Wendt, Alexander "Anarchy Is What States Make of It." *International Organization* 46, no. 2 (Spring 1992).
59. Zafar, Shaista Shaheen. "Britain's Role in the Rann of Kutch Dispute." *Journal of European Studies* 24, no. 2. (2008): 250–275.
60. Zalta, Edward N., ed. "Political Realism in International Relations." In *The Stanford Encyclopedia of Philosophy*, Summer 2013 ed., edited by Edward N. Zalta. Last accessed October 23, 2014. http://plato.stanford.edu/archives/sum2013/entries/realism-intl-relations/

# Books

1. Absher, Kenneth Michael. *Mind-sets and Missiles: A First Hand Account of the Cuban Missile Crisis*. South Carolina: CreateSpace Independent Publishing Platform, 2009.
2. Ahmer, Moonis, ed. *Conflict Resolution Research in South Asia*. Karachi: Department of International Relations, University of Karachi, 2010.
3. Allison, Graham, and Philip Zelikow. *Essence of Decision: Explaining the Cuban Missile Crisis*. New York: Longman, 1999.
4. Arif, General K.M. *Khaki Shadows: Pakistan 1947–1997*. Karachi: Oxford University Press, 2001.
5. Ash, Robert B. *Basic Probability Theory*. Mineola, NY: Dover Publications, 1970.
6. Ayson, Robert. *Thomas Schelling and the Nuclear Age: Strategy as Social Science*. New York: Routledge, 2004.
7. Bahl, Y. *Kargil Blunder: Pakistan Plight, India's Victory*. New Delhi: Manes Publications, 2008.
8. Bajpai, Kanti P., P.R. Chari, Pervaiz Iqbal Cheema, Stephen P. Cohen, and Sumit Ganguly. *Brasstacks and Beyond: Perception and Management of Crisis in South Asia*. Lahore: Vanguard Books, 1995.
9. Barros, James, ed. *The United Nations: Past, Present, and Future*. New York: Free Press, 1972.
10. Basrur, Rajesh. *Minimum Deterrence and India's Nuclear Security*. Stanford, CA: Stanford University Press, 2006.
11. Bhattacherjee, Anol. *Social Science Research: Principles, Methods, and Practices*. Textbooks Collection, Book 3, 2012.
12. Barry, Buzan. *People, States, and Fear: The National Security Problems in International Relations*. Essck: Wheatsheaf Book, 1983.
13. Barros, James, ed. *The United Nations: Past, Present, and Future*. New York: Free Press, 1972.
14. Beck, Lewis White, ed. *Perpetual Peace*. New York: Macmillan, 1957.

15. Brown, David. *Palmerston and the Politics of Foreign Policy, 1846–1855*. Manchester: Manchester University Press, 2002.
16. Chakma, Bhumitra. *Pakistan's Nuclear Weapons*. London: Routledge, 2009.
17. Chamber, Michael R., ed. *South Asia in 2020: Future Strategic Balances and Alliances*. Carlisle: Strategic Studies Institute Monograph, US Army War College, 2002.
18. Chari, P.R., Pervaiz Iqbal Cheema, and Stephen P. Cohen. *Four Crises and a Peace Process: American Engagement in South Asia*. Washington, DC: Brookings Institution Press, 2007.
19. Cheema, Pervaiz Iqbal, Rashid Ahmed Khan, and Khalid Chandio, ed. *Pakistan-India Peace Process: The Way Forward*. Islamabad: Policy Research Institute, 2010.
20. Cheema, Pervaiz Iqbal. *The Armed Forces of Pakistan*. New York: New York University Press, 1996.
21. Cheema, Zafar Iqbal. *Indian Nuclear Deterrence: Its Evolution, Development, and Implications for South Asian Security*. Karachi: Oxford University Press, 2010.
22. Clavell, James. *The Art of War*. Lahore: Combine Printers, 1983.
23. Cloughly, Brian. *A History of Pakistan Army; Wars and Insurrections*. 2nd ed. Rawalpindi: Army Education Publishing House, 2001.
24. Dalrymple, William. "The Great Divide: The Violent Legacy of Indian Partition." *The New Yorker*, 2015.
25. Davis, Zachary S. *The India-Pakistan Military Standoff: Crisis and Escalation in South Asia*. New York: Palgrave Macmillan, 2011.
26. Derian, J. Den, ed. *International Theory: Critical Investigations*. London: Macmillan, 1995.
27. Delpech, Therese. *Nuclear Deterrence in the 21st Century*. Santa Monica: RAND Corporation, 2012.
28. Dixit, J.N. *India-Pakistan in War & Peace*. London: Routledge, 2002.
29. Dubois, Didier, and Henri Prade, *Possibility Theory and Its Applications: Where Do We Stand?* Toulouse: University of Paul Sabatier, 2011. Toulouse Cedex 09, France.
30. Freedman, Lawrence. *The Evolution of Nuclear Strategy*. 3rd ed. London: Palgrave Macmillan, 2003.
31. Freedman, Lawrence. *Deterrence*. Cambridge: Polity Press, 2004.
32. Ganguly, Sumit. *Conflict Unending; India-Pakistan Tension since 1947*. New York: Columbia University Press, 2001.
33. Ganguly, Sumit, and Kapoor S. Paul. *India, Pakistan, and the Bomb: Debating the Nuclear Stability in South Asia*. New Delhi: Viking Penguin, 2010.
34. Garthoff, Raymond L. *Reflections on the Cuban Missile Crisis*. Washington, DC: Brookings Institution, 1987.
35. Greene, Robert. *The 33 Strategies of War*. New Delhi: Viva Books, 2006.
36. Hassan, Javed. (Brig). *India: A Study Profile*. Rawalpindi: Army Education Press, 1990.
37. Hussain, Ijaz. *Kashmir Dispute: An International Law Perspective*. Islamabad: Instant Print System, 1998.
38. Iqbal, Javid Dr. *Ideology of Pakistan*. Lahore: Sang-e-Meel Publications, 2005.
39. Jackson, Robert, and Georg Sorensen. *Introduction to International Relations: Theories and Approaches*. 3rd ed. Oxford: Oxford University Press, 2007.

40. Kegley Jr. Chrles, W. Wittkopf, and Eugene R. *World Politics: Trends & Transformations*. 9th ed. Belmont CA: Thompson, Wadsworth, 2004.
41. Khan Saira. *Nuclear Weapons and Conflict Transformation: The Case of India-Pakistan*. London: Routledge, 2009.
42. Khan, Zulfqar, ed. *Nuclear Pakistan; Strategic Dimension*. Karachi: Oxford University Press, 2011.
43. Kissinger, Henry. *Nuclear Weapons and Foreign Policy*. New York: Harper and Brothers, 1957.
44. Kohli, Atul. *The State and Poverty in India*. London: Cambridge University Press, 1987.
45. Krepon, Michael, and Nate Cohn. *Crises in South Asia: Trends and Potential Consequences*. Washington, DC: The Henry L. Stimson Center, 2011.
46. Kreppon, Michael, Rodney W. Jones, and Ziad Haider, ed. *Escalation Control and the Nuclear Option in South Asia*. Washington, DC: The Stimson Center, 2004.
47. Keohane, Robert O., and Joseph Nye. *Power and Interdependence*. 3rd ed. New York: Longman, 2001.
48. Lamb, Alastair. *Birth of a Tragedy: Kashmir 1947*. London: Oxford University Press, 1994.
49. Lamb, Alastair. *Kashmir: A Disputed Legacy, 1846–1990*. Pakistan: Oxford University Press, 1991.
50. Laski, Harold J. *The State in Theory and Practice*. London: George Allen and Unwin Ltd., 1935.
51. Lavoy, Peter R., ed. *Asymmetric Warfare in South Asia: The Causes and Consequences of the Kargil Conflict*. Cambridge: Cambridge University Press, 2009.
52. Lodhi, Maleeha. *Pakistan: Beyond the "Crisis State."* Karachi: Oxford University Press, 2011.
53. Louw, Michael H. *National Security*. Pretoria: University of Pretoria, 1978.
54. Malik, Hafeez, ed. *Dilemmas of National Security and Cooperation in India and Pakistan*. New York: St Martin's Press, 1993.
55. Malik, V.P. General (Retd.). *Kargil: From Surprise to Victory*. New Delhi: Harper Collins, 2006.
56. Matinuddin, Kamal. *The Nuclearisation of South Asia*. Karachi: Oxford University Press, 2002.
57. Mazari, Shireen M. *The Kargil Conflict 1999: Separating Fact from Fiction*. Islamabad: Ferozsons, 2003.
58. Mingst, Karen A. *Essential of International Relations*. 4th ed. New York: W.W. Norton, 2008.
59. Mohan, Raja C. *The Shaping of India's New Foreign Policy*. New Delhi: Penguin, 2003.
60. Morgan, Patrick M. *Deterrence Now*. Cambridge: Cambridge University Press, 2003.
61. Morgenthau, Hans J. *Scientific Man vs Power Politics*. Chicago: University of Chicago Press, 1952.
62. Morgenthau, Hans J. *Politics among Nations: The Struggle for Power and Peace*. 5th rev. ed. New York: Alfred A. Knopf, 1973.
63. Musa, Mohammad, General (Retd.). *My Vision: India-Pakistan War 1965*. Lahore: WAJIDALIS, 1983.
64. Mroz, John E. *Beyond Security: Private Perceptions among Arabs and Israelis*. New York: International Peace Academy, 1980.
65. Musharraf, Pervez. *In the Line of Fire: A Memoir*. London: Simon & Shuster, 2006. 66.

66. Nayak, Polly, and Michael Krepon, *US Crisis Management in South Asia's Twin Peaks Crisis*. Washington, DC: The Stimson Center, 2006.
67. Organski, A.F.K., and Jacek Kugler, *The War Ledger*. Chicago: University of Chicago Press, 1980.
68. Osgood, Charles E. *An Alternative to War or Surrender*. Chicago: University of Illinois, 1962.
69. Paul, T.V. *The India-Pakistan Conflict: An Enduring Rivalry*. Cambridge: Cambridge University Press, 2006.
70. Paul, T.V., James J. Wirtz, and Michel Fortmann, ed. *Balance of Power: Theory and Practice in the 21st Century*. Stanford, CA: Stanford University Press, 2004.
71. Pamidi, G.G. *Possibility of a Nuclear War in Asia: An Indian Perspective*. New Delhi: Vij Books, 2012.
72. Perkovich, George. *India's Nuclear Bomb: The Impact of Global Proliferation*. Berkley, CA: University of California Press, 1999.
73. Pervez, Shoaib. *Security Community in South Asia: India-Pakistan*. New York: Routledge, 2013.
74. Raghavan, V.R. Lt Gen (Retd.). *Siachen—A Conflict without End*. New Delhi: Penguin Books, 2002.
75. Riedel, Bruce. *Deadly Embrace: Pakistan, America, and the Future of the Global Jihad*. Washington, DC: Bookings Institution Press, 2011.
76. Robert, Ayson. *Thomas Schelling and the Nuclear Age: Strategy as Social Science*. New York: Routledge, 2004.
77. Sagan, Scott D., and Kenneth N. Waltz. *The Spread of Nuclear Weapons: A Debate Renewed*. New York: W.W. Norton, 2003.
78. Sagen, D. Scott, ed. *Inside Nuclear South Asia*. London: Stanford University Press, 2009.
79. Schellenberg, James A. *Conflict Resolution: Theory, Research and Practice*. New York: State University of New York Press, 1996.
80. Shamsi, Zia Ul Haque. *Nuclear Deterrence and Conflict Management Between India and Pakistan*. New York: Peter Lang, 2020.
81. Shamsi, Zia Ul Haque. *South Asia Needs Hybrid Peace*. New York: Peter Lang, 2022.
82. Shamsi, Zia Ul Haque. *Understanding Sun Tzu and the Art of Hybrid War*. New York: Peter Lang, 2023.
83. Singh, Dr Anil Kumar. *India's Security Concerns in the Indian Ocean Region*. New Delhi: Har-Anand Publications, 2003.
84. Stoessinger, Johng. *Why Nations Go to War*. New York: St. Martin's Press, 1990.
85. Tellis, Ashley J., Fair, Christine C., and Medby, Jamison Jo. *Limited Conflicts under the Nuclear Umbrella*. RAND Report, 2001.
86. Wallensteen, Peter. *Understanding Conflict Resolution*. 3rd ed. London: SAGE Publications, 2012.
87. Waltz, Kenneth. *Theory of International Politics*. New York: McGraw Hill, 1979.
88. Waltz, Kenneth, and Scott D. Sagen. *The Spread of Nuclear Weapons: A Debate Renewed*. New York: W. W. Norton, 1995.
89. Waslekar, Sundeep. *A Hand Book for Conflict Resolution in South Asia*. New Delhi: Konark Publishers, 1996.

90. Windsor, Philip. *Strategic thinking; An introduction and Farewell*, edited by Mats Berdaled, Spyros Economides. Boulder: Lynne Reiner Publisher, 2006.
91. Wittner, Lawrence S. *Confronting the Bomb: A Short History of the World Disarmament Movement*. Stanford: Stanford University Press, 2014.
92. Wolpert, Stanley. *Shameful Flight: The Last Years of the British Empire in India*. Oxford: Oxford University Press, 2006. 93.
93. Wolpert, Stanley. *Jinnah of Pakistan*. Karachi: Oxford University Press, 1984.
94. Wolpert, Stanley. *India and Pakistan: Continued Conflict or Cooperation?* London: University of California Press, 2010.
95. Ziring, Lawrence. *Pakistan in the Twentieth Century: A Political History*. Karachi: Oxford University Press, 1997.
96. Zalta, Edward N., ed. *The Stanford Encyclopedia of Philosophy*. Summer ed. Stanford: Stanford University, 2013.

www.ingramcontent.com/pod-product-compliance
Ingram Content Group UK Ltd.
Pitfield, Milton Keynes, MK11 3LW, UK
UKHW022240230426
12048UKWH00018BA/1363